CODING
HTML · CSS
JAVASCRIPT
MADE EASY

Publisher and Creative Director: Nick Wells
Project Editor: Polly Prior
Art Director and Layout Design: Mike Spender
Digital Design and Production: Chris Herbert
Copy Editors: Katharine Baker and Anna Groves
Technical Editors: Adam Crute and Chris Brown
Proofreader: Dawn Laker
Indexer: Helen Snaith
Screenshots: Frederic Johnson and Adam Crute

FLAME TREE PUBLISHING
6 Melbray Mews
London SW6 3NS
United Kingdom

www.flametreepublishing.com
First published 2016

18 20 19
3 5 7 9 10 8 6 4

A CIP record for this book is available from the British Library upon request.

ISBN 978-1-78664-061-1

Printed in China | Created, Developed & Produced in the United Kingdom

The content in this book was originally published in *Coding HTML & CSS Basics* and *Coding Javascript Basics*.

All non-screenshot pictures are courtesy of Shutterstock and © the following photographers: iinspiration 1; baitong333 3; marekuliasz 4, 14,
46; ronstik 4, 40; Rawpixel 5, 9, 21, 32, 70, 90, 111, 182; agsandrew 5, 112; vchal 6, 132; McIek 6, 146, 153, 169, 176, 204; iunewind 6, 170;
wongwean 7, 202; patpitchaya 7, 26, 117, 208, 232; Raywoo 8, 44; NakoPhotography 12; Jane Kelly 13, 137, 139; Ai825 16, 69; Dxinerz-Pvt-
Ltd 19; Pressmaster 22, 160; Gonzalo Aragon 24; Syda Productions 25; MoneyRender 23; Monkey Business Images 30; fotogestoeber 35;
Miha Perosa 47; billdayone 49; Sergey Nivens 54, 116; wavebreakmedia 61, 90, 126, 252; Hamara 64; Andrey_Popov 66; winui 73; everything
possible 76; Chukcha 78; baranq 81; Ingvar Bjork 89; Antonio Gravante 92; hanss 100; 3d brained 105; SiuWing 111; MPFphotography 125;
Morrowind 134, 149; bikeriderlondon 136; gdainti 58, 137, 139, 253; pogonici 145; Dragana Gerasimoski 152; Katharina Wittfeld 157;
StockLite 162; Goodluz 167; Matej Kastelic 175; isak55 179; Pavel Ignatov 186; mimagephotography 205; Gwoeii 214; Pixza Studio 215;
ra2studio 219; Lincoln Rogers 226; spaxiax 239; Dragon Images 241; NicoElNino 245; Danielala 251.

CODING
HTML · CSS
JAVASCRIPT
MADE EASY

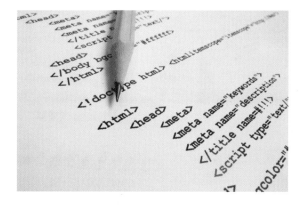

ADAM CRUTE & FREDERIC JOHNSON

FLAME TREE
PUBLISHING

CONTENTS

New to coding? Then this introduction to HTML and CSS is a must-read to start you off. It will tell you exactly what you should know before you begin reading this book, to get the most out of it. Find out what HTML tags and elements are, and how they become the essential backbone of any website. Also learn how CSS creates the look of a website, allowing you to apply style rules to make each page look professional or aesthetically pleasing.

This chapter takes HTML and CSS further, expanding on the points of the previous chapter to help you gain greater knowledge. In particular, it looks at HTML elements including headers, footers and other structural elements. The chapter then moves on to CSS class selectors and text-based elements, including how to create hyperlinks and lists.

CREATING WEBSITES 70

Learn how to plan, build and style a website in this chapter. With easy to follow step-by-step instructions and, with everything you've learned already, by the end of it you'll have your unique website up and running online. Additionally, this chapter shows you how to style your web pages with CSS and add a blog to your website using WordPress.

IMAGES, VIDEO & OTHER ENHANCEMENTS 90

By adding images, audio and video to your site you will take it to another level, making it more engaging and thereby increasing the number of people likely to visit. This chapter will take you through working with images, audio and video, including the best file formats to use and how to add each of them to your website. As well as this, the basics of HTML5, CSS transitions and CSS keyframes are all covered here.

ADVANCED HTML & CSS CODING 112

Take your knowledge even further in this chapter and learn about character entities, adaptive layouts and Responsive Web Design (RWD). RWD is important if you want your website to look good on all kinds of devices, including smartphones and tablets, as well as desktops. Grasp how to make the most of your website on mobile browsers, as well as which browsers are best to support. Also included here is a troubleshooting guide.

MEET JAVASCRIPT 132

Reader, meet JavaScript - JavaScript, meet reader. Find out here what exactly what JavaScript is and how it can improve your website. This chapter also tackles the basics of writing scripts and what happens when a browser encounters JavaScript. By the end of the chapter you will be able to write and execute basic JavaScript.

DATA IN JAVASCRIPT 146

In this chapter, it is explained exactly what data is and how to work with it in JavaScript. Different types of data such as primitive data, including Booleans and numbers, as well as reference data types, including arrays are covered. On top of this differences between each data type and what they can help you achieve are explained.

ANATOMY OF JAVASCRIPT . . . 170

Here, we explore how JavaScript is structured. This includes script syntax, how to put comments into your codes to help others to understand them, as well as looking at expressions and operators and how they work together to manipulate data. Statements are also covered, including conditional and loop statements.

FUNCTIONS & CLASSES OF JAVASCRIPT

Now that we have covered statements it is important to look at creating reusable code using functions, and how to create a named function. We also look at why it is important to use namespaces, to avoid the risk of creating name clashes. We then introduce Object Oriented Programming; explain how classes are used in JavaScript; and give instructions on how to create a main class, a very useful ability to have.

THE DOM & EVENTS OF JAVASCRIPT

In this final chapter, we look at the last pieces in the JavaScript jigsaw: the Document Object Model, or DOM, and events. Javascript's DOM classes allow us to manipulate an already loaded page, which opens up a whole realm of possibilities. We explore how to retrieve and add elements to the DOM and then move on to looking at events and event listeners.

USEFUL WEBSITES & FURTHER READING

INDEX

FOREWORD

We live in a connected world. We share news, stories and images; our noblest aspirations and darkest nightmares (not to mention rather a lot of cat pictures) criss-cross the globe at an ever-increasing rate, whilst our appetite to consume this infinite variation of human thought (and cute cat pictures) seems boundless.

The conduit for all of this information, the pipes through which the data flows – the enchanted loom through which global culture intertwines and advances – is the internet. Learning to speak the language of the internet, then, is both empowering and rewarding.

Many people believe that programming is hard to learn; nothing could be further from the truth. If you know that 1 + 2 = 3, and that you have to open the fridge door before you take out the milk, then you can program!

Of course, mastering any language – human or computer – requires dedicated study over an extended period of time. But just as it's simple to learn enough French to communicate with the locals on a holiday to Paris, so it is easy to get to grips with the basics of most computer languages.

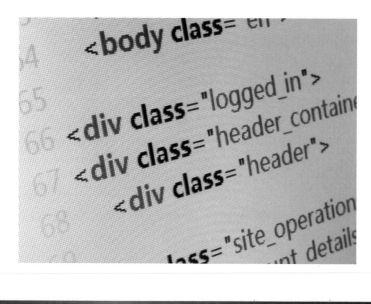

The languages of the internet – HTML, CSS and JavaScript – are amongst the simplest languages one can learn, as well as being the most useful and ubiquitous. This book is only an introduction to these languages, yet will empower you with the ability to create your own vibrant and exciting websites from scratch.

Don't be scared, it's easy. Turn the page and see for yourself...

Adam Crute

INTRODUCTION

Nowadays, everyone uses the internet, from hobbyists to big business. If you want to promote yourself, a product or simply let people know about your passion, a website gives you a window on the world. It is the go-to destination to find out more information about absolutely anything.

HTML AND CSS

Now you know why you need a website, how do you go about building one? The core technologies behind every site on the web are HTML (HyperText Markup Language) and CSS (Cascading Style Sheets). This book reveals exactly how they work, what they can do and, more importantly, shows you how to create your very own website.

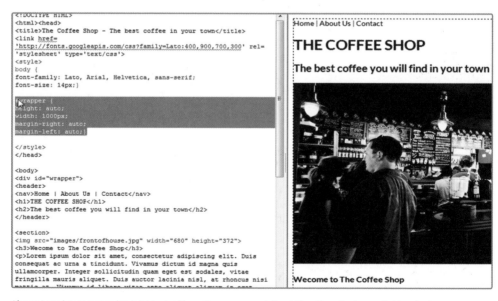

Above: Learn how to turn code into internet gold; creating your own website might not be as hard as you first imagined.

GO FURTHER

The advice doesn't stop at simply creating your website: learn how to get your website onto the internet, find out how you can buy your very own .com name, create a blog with WordPress, discover some advanced CSS techniques and learn simple JavaScript language.

STEP-BY-STEP

The process of building a website and learning new languages can seem like a daunting task. But this book rises to the challenge and demonstrates the process through a selection of step-by-step guides. These provide easy-to-follow instructions which will guide you through some of the most important building blocks of a website.

EXPERT GUIDANCE

Should all not go according to plan, our helpful troubleshooting guide will help get you back on track, and our Further Reading guide will point you in the direction of where to go next.

CODE EXAMPLES

When showing examples of HTML, CSS and JavaScript code we will use text that looks `like this`. When we want to indicate that something would be written in a code block but that we haven't shown it in the example, we would bold the text as well, like this: `header {`**`style rule`**`}`. You wouldn't type 'style rule' into the code – rather, we're showing you where the style rule would go.

Hot Tip

In addition to the more substantial step-by-steps, there is a collection of Hot Tip guides. These offer quick, handy hints as well as advice to add flourishes to the final website.

THE FORMATION OF JAVASCRIPT

The JavaScript language has been with us since the very earliest days of the World Wide Web. In its early days it was merely one face in a crowd, one of many languages and technologies vying for the attention and evangelism of the web development community.

UNIVERSAL LANGUAGE

Over the years, many such technologies have come into fashion before falling from grace for one reason or another, but not so with JavaScript. Thanks largely to a combination of flexibility and ubiquitousness, JavaScript is now *the* principal scripting language of the internet.

A STEP UP FROM HTML/CSS

Despite JavaScript's at-times esoteric nature, it is the perfect language to use for learning about coding in general. This book is aimed at people who are quite new to writing code and programming. You may be completely new to HTML, CSS and JavaScript; you may have spent some time with HTML and CSS and want to refresh your knowledge and learn about JavaScript; or you may have tinkered with a bit of scripting and want to formalize and expand on that knowledge. You may even be an experienced programmer who has never used JavaScript and wants a quick overview to get started.

GO-TO PRIMER

There's no getting away from the fact that JavaScript is a deep subject, so much so that no single book can tell you all there is to know about the language and what it can achieve. What *this* book aims to do, then, is to deliver a wide-ranging overview of the JavaScript language, and give you sufficient understanding to be able to add your own simple scripts and interactions to your pages. It is also perfect as a primer for further studies in coding with JavaScript.

Online Samples

You can download completed versions of the JavaScript code examples and additional notes. To do so, visit www.flametreepublishing.com/book-samples.html.

Hot Tips

Look out for the Hot Tips that give you helpful tips about the many shortcuts and quick techniques available in JavaScript.

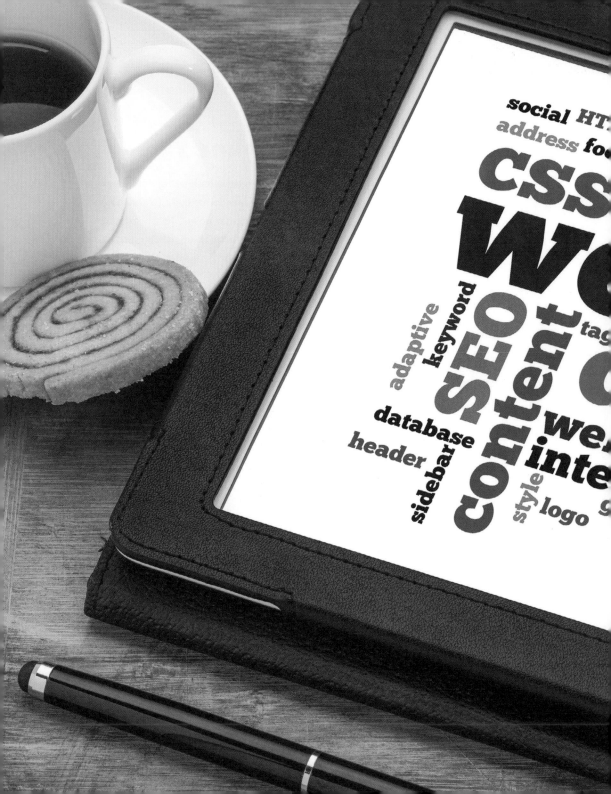

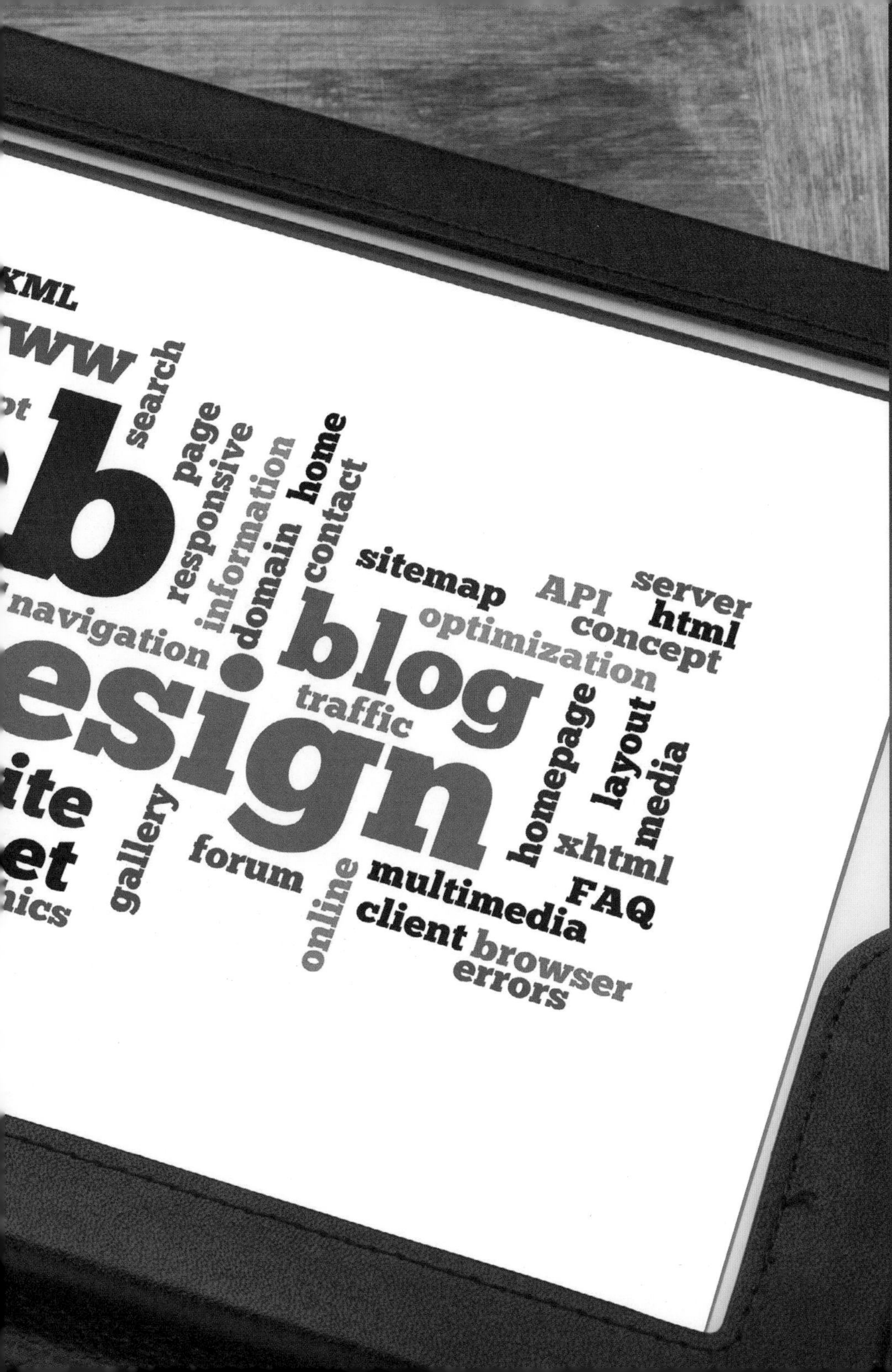

ALL ABOUT HTML & CSS

AN INTRODUCTION TO HTML

HTML is the most important component for building websites, web apps and anything else that's delivered via the web. But what is it and what does it do?

WHAT IS HTML?

HTML, or HyperText Markup Language to give it its official title, is the framework upon which all websites are built. If a website were a house, HTML would be the bricks and mortar.

HTML consists of **elements**, the bricks in our hypothetical house. An element starts and ends with something called a **tag** – the mortar, if you will. There are many different elements, each of which has a specific intended use. For example, the video element is used to – can you guess? – yes, place a video on a web page. When your choices of elements are put together in a suitable order you have a web page!

```
1    <h1>HTML is a collection of elements</h1>
2    <h2>These elements are demarked by tags</h2>
3    <p>Each element has a name - it is included in the tag</p>
4    <p>Whatever appears between the opening and closing tags is the content of the element</p>
5
```

Above: HTML is made up of elements, demarked by tags.

WHAT DOES HTML LOOK LIKE?

HTML is nothing more than plain text. If we were creating the aforementioned video element we would write an **opening tag**, `<video>`, and a matching **closing tag**, `</video>`. As you can see, the opening tag starts with '<', states the element name, and then finishes with '>'. The closing tag follows the same pattern, but we insert a '/' before the element name. When a web browser encounters this element it creates a video player on the page. Simple, huh?

What's Inside An Element

So, what goes between those tags? In most circumstances the answer is text and/or other elements. This means that HTML has a nested structure of elements within elements. Incidentally, many developers indent lines of code to reflect this nesting.

```
1   <!DOCTYPE HTML>
2
3   <html>
4
5       <head>
6           <title>My Page</title>
7       </head>
8
9       <body>
10          <header>
11              <h1>A Page All About Me</h1>
12          </header>
13
14          <section>
15              <h2>What I'm thinking now</h2>
16              <p>Lorem ipsum dolor sit amet, consectetuer adipiscing elit. Sed sagittis ante malesuada velit.
    Curabitur suscipit. Suspendisse quis nibh aliquam sem pulvinar sollicitudin. Etiam venenatis. Curabitur
    luctus.</p>
17              <p>Nunc venenatis lacus molestie sapien. Maecenas elementum aliquet velit. Ut eget mauris sed leo
    scelerisque lacinia. Nunc arcu magna, mollis id, ornare ac, pharetra sit amet, purus. Aliquam luctus
    consectetuer dolor.</p>
18          </section>
19
20      </body>
21
22  </html>
23
```

Above: Indenting lines of code highlights the nested structure of your elements.

MODIFYING ELEMENTS

Whilst all HTML elements have an intended use, nearly all can be modified in various ways too. For example, we may want to change the dimensions of a video player or the font size of a heading.

Elements are modified by adjusting the **attributes** of the element, and this is done in the opening tag:

```
<video width="720" height="360">
```

As you can see, an attribute name is declared within the opening tag, is followed by '='
and then a **value** wrapped inside quote marks.

Components of HTML

- **Element**: The basic building block of HTML.

- **Tag**: Defines the start and end of an element.

- **Attribute**: Modifies the behaviour and appearance of an element.

> ## Hot Tip
>
> **When using quote marks in HTML you can use single ' or double ", but it is vital to be consistent in which you use.**

```
15
16    <video width="640" width="360" src="vids/introvid.mp4"> </video>
17
18    <section lang="en">
19        <article id="article_01">
20            <h2 class="underlinedText">Lorem ipsum dolor sit amet</h2>
21            <p class="redText">Sed sagittis ante malesuada velit. Curabitur suscipit.</p>
22        </article>
23    </section>
24
25
```

Above: Attributes allow you to modify an element.

DOING THINGS WITH STYLE

In old versions of HTML a plethora of different attributes existed for controlling the visual appearance of elements. What's more, different elements had wildly varying sets of attributes that they recognized. Remembering all of the connotations and variations was a nightmare, and so the `style` attribute was developed.

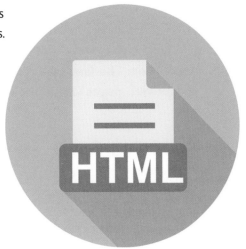

Obey The Rules

The value assigned to a `style` attribute is called a **style rule** and this consists of one or more **style commands**. A style command is a pairing of a **style property** and a value to be applied to that property, for example:

```
<body style="color:green; font-weight:bold;">.
```

Each style property name (`color` and `font-weight` in this example) is followed by a colon ':', then the value to be assigned to that property, and finally a semicolon ';'.

```
8
9       <body>
10
11          <header style="font-size:18px; color:blue;">
12              <h1 style="font-weight:bold;">HTML and CSS Basics</h1>
13              <h2 style="font-size:14px;">Learn the language of the Internet</h2>
14          </header>
15
16          |
17          <video width="640" width="360" src="vids/introvid.mp4"></video>
18
```

Above: The style attribute allows you to add inline styling to an element.

AN INTRODUCTION TO CSS

If HTML is the bricks and mortar of a house, then CSS provides the decoration. The language is simple but packs a big punch, and without it your web pages would look awful.

WHAT IS CSS?

We've already looked at adding a style rule to an element's `style` attribute. This is called **Inline** styling – it works, but has an inherent problem: if you want to change, say, the font of all of your text headings then you have to edit the `font-family` style property in *every* occurrence of a heading element. This is where **CSS** comes into the picture.

```
2
3   <html>
4
5       <head>
6           <title>All About HTML</title>
7       </head>
8
9       <body>
10
11          <header style="font-size:18px; color:blue;">
12              <h1 style="font-weight:bold;">HTML and CSS Basics</h1>
13              <h2 style="font-size:14px;">Learn the language of the
    Internet</h2>
14          </header>
15
16
```

HTML and CSS Basics

Learn the language of the Internet

Lorem ipsum dolor sit amet

Sed sagittis ante malesuada velit. Curabitur suscipit. Suspendisse quis nibh aliquam sem pulvinar sollicitudin. Etiam venenatis! Curabitur luctus. Nunc venenatis lacus molestie sapien. Maecenas elementum aliquet velit. Ut eget mauris sed leo scelerisque lacinia. Nunc arcu magna, mollis id, ornare ac, pharetra sit amet, purus. Aliquam luctus consectetuer dolor. In placerat, diam et suscipit posuere, lacus orci vestibulum libero, vulputate faucibus felis leo sit amet elit. Sed hendrerit felis non urna. Donec interdum dui at est. Pellentesque sit amet urna et nunc lobortis egestas. Vestibulum et orci.

```
3   <html>
4
5       <head>
6           <title>All About HTML</title>
7       </head>
8
9       <body>
10
11          <header style="font-size:24px; color:red;">
12              <h1 style="font-weight:bold;">HTML and CSS Basics</h1>
13              <h2 style="font-size:14px; background-color:black;">
    Learn the language of the Internet</h2>
14          </header>
15
16
17
18          <section id="sect1">
19              <article id="article_01" lang="en">
20                  <h2 class="italicText">Lorem ipsum dolor sit amet</
```

HTML and CSS Basics

Learn the language of the Internet

Lorem ipsum dolor sit amet

Sed sagittis ante malesuada velit. Curabitur suscipit. Suspendisse quis nibh aliquam sem pulvinar sollicitudin. Etiam venenatis! Curabitur luctus. Nunc venenatis lacus molestie sapien. Maecenas elementum aliquet velit. Ut eget mauris sed leo scelerisque lacinia. Nunc arcu magna, mollis id, ornare ac, pharetra sit amet, purus. Aliquam luctus consectetuer dolor. In placerat, diam et suscipit posuere, lacus orci vestibulum libero, vulputate faucibus felis leo sit amet elit. Sed hendrerit felis non urna. Donec interdum dui at est. Pellentesque sit amet urna et nunc lobortis egestas. Vestibulum et orci.

Above: Making a change to inline style rules can be a fiddly process.

CSS stands for Cascading Style Sheets. It provides the means of separating page content from page appearance, and of applying a style rule to more than one element at a time. A key benefit of this is that any changes made to a CSS style rule will affect all elements that are associated with that rule.

```
25
26   header {
27        position:relative;
28        width:1024px;
29        height:130px;
30        margin:0px auto 0px auto;
31        padding:0px;
32        background-color:#778081;
33        border:none;
34        border-bottom:2px solid #FD5F12;
35   }
36
37   nav {
38        position:relative;
39        width:788px;
40        height:30px;
41        margin:0px auto 0px auto;
42        padding:0px 118px 0px 118px;
43        background-color:#D9D9D9;
44        border:none;
45        border-bottom:1px solid #FD5F12;
46   }
47
```

Above: CSS code comprises selectors and style rules. Notice how indenting the code assists with legibility.

WHAT DOES CSS LOOK LIKE?

Like HTML, CSS is plain text written with a specific structure. CSS code is comprised of **selectors** that identify the HTML element(s) that the subsequent style rule will be applied to. The style rule itself is wrapped in curly brackets, '{' and '}'.

Selection of Selectors

Selectors can take a number of different forms, but in this book we will only focus on three of them: **Type**, **ID** and **Class** selectors. The simplest of these is the Type selector (we'll return to the others later). It consists of nothing more than the name of the HTML element that will receive the selector's style rule. For example, a p selector will target all instances of <p> elements.

WHY CASCADING?

When writing HTML we create a nested structure in which every element is nested within another element. This means that every element has a **parent** element – the element in which a given element is nested – and most elements have **child** element(s), i.e., the element(s) nested within a given element.

```
12
13
14        <section>
15            <h3>Lorem Ipsum</h3>
16        </section>
17
18
```

Above: HTML's nested structure is expressed in terms of ancestry. Here <h3> is the child of <section>, and <section> is the parent of <h3>.

When a web browser **renders** (draws) an element in a web page, it has to assess which style rule to apply to that element. But what if it were rendering an element that displays text, such as <h3>, but no font-family property had been defined in the style rule applied to that element – how does the browser determine which font to use? The answer is that it looks to the parent element and copies the font-family property from there.

If a parent element also lacks a specific style property then that property would be inherited from the parent's parent, and so on. Ultimately we have a 'cascade' of style properties in which a property applied to one element will be inherited by the children of that element, unless a child specifically overrides it with a new rule of its own. When this happens the properties of the new rule are passed into the inheritance chain.

Hot Tip

The structure of CSS is simple, but beware: CSS is unforgiving of mistakes.

Components of CSS

- **Selector**: Targets the HTML element(s) that style rules will be applied to.

- **Style command**: Specifies a style property and assigns a value to it (aka a 'property-value pair').

- **Style rule**: A collection of style properties and their associated values.

Right: A complete CSS style sheet containing multiple selectors and style rules.

```
1
2   body {
3       position:relative;
4       background-color:#FD5F12;
5       margin:0px;
6       padding:0px;
7       width:100%;
8       height:100%;
9   }
10
11  #pageBgFill {
12      position:fixed;
13      width:1024px;
14      left:0px;
15      right:0px;
16      top:0px;
17      bottom:0px;
18      margin:0px auto 0px auto;
19      background-color:#D9D9D9;
20  }
21
22  header {
23      position:relative;
24      width:1024px;
25      height:130px;
26      margin:0px auto 0px auto;
27      padding:0px;
28      background-color:#778081;
29      border:none;
30      border-bottom:2px solid #FD5F12;
31  }
32
33  nav {
34      position:relative;
35      width:788px;
36      height:30px;
37      margin:0px auto 0px auto;
38      padding:0px 118px 0px 118px;
39      background-color:#D9D9D9;
40      border:none;
41      border-bottom:1px solid #FD5F12;
```

ESSENTIAL ELEMENTS

As we have learned, an HTML document is made up of a structure of elements, each of which performs a certain role. This document acts like a set of instructions for a web browser, telling it what to draw where. Let's look at the essential elements required by all documents.

THE DOCTYPE DECLARATION

There are a couple of different dialects of HTML that are currently in use – HTML5, the most up-to-date, and XHTML. This book is concerned only with the former, so suffice to say that

```
1  <!DOCTYPE HTML>
2
3
4
5
```

Above: All HTML documents start with a DOCTYPE declaration; this is the declaration for HTML5.

XHTML exists and isn't drastically different from HTML5 – in fact you'd struggle to notice the difference if you didn't know what to look for!

A web browser, however, *has* to be able to tell the difference so that it knows how to render the page. To this end *all* HTML documents start with a **DOCTYPE** declaration. HTML5's declaration is `<!DOCTYPE HTML>`. This easy-to-remember declaration must appear at the top of every HTML5 web page that you create.

THE HTML ELEMENT

If all elements have a parent element then somewhere down the chain there must be a progenitor or starting point; this is the special `<html>` element. All HTML documents include one – and only one – such element. All of the other elements that comprise the web page are nested within this `<html>` element.

```
1   <!DOCTYPE HTML>
2
3   <html>
4
5   </html>
6
7
8   |
```

Above: All HTML documents contain one `<html>` element: no more, no less.

```
1   <!DOCTYPE HTML>
2
3   <html>
4
5        <head>
6
7        </head>
8
9        <body>
10
11       </body>
12
13  </html>
14
```

Above: The <html> element
always contains a <head>
and a <body> element.

HEAD AND BODY ELEMENTS

The special <html> element always has two child elements,
no more, no less: <head> and <body>, in that order.
Without these two elements a web page will not work
properly (if at all).

The <head> element contains information about the web
page, such as its title (shown at the top of the browser
window), the text that will appear in search listings, links
to other resources, and so on. Nothing within the <head>
is rendered into the visible part of the web page.

The <body> element takes care of the actual visible content
of your page, i.e. the elements that produce visual output on
the rendered web page. Typically you add elements to the
<body> in the layout order they will appear on-screen.

CODE COMMENTS

Practically all programming languages provide a facility for adding **comments** to your code, and HTML is no different. Their main use is to add notes, explanations and reminders inside a document, all of which will be ignored by the browser. They can be especially important if you are working on a large website and/or are collaborating with other developers. Best practice, then, is to use comments liberally and freely – you'll be glad you did if you ever have to revisit a page you wrote months previously. An HTML comment looks like this:

```
<!-- This is an HTML comment -->.
```

Hot Tip

Use comments to disable a line or section of code without having to delete it altogether. This really helps when experimenting with ideas or bug hunting.

```
5      <head>
6
7          <!--TO DO: Come up with a better title for the page -->
8          <title>My Page</title>
9      </head>
10
11     <body>
12         |<header>
13             <h1>A Page All About Me</h1>
14         </header>
15
16         <section>
17             <h2>What I'm thinking now</h2>
18
19             <!-- Placeholder text...-->
20             <p>Lorem ipsum dolor sit amet, consectetuer adipiscing elit. Sed sagittis ante malesuada velit.
   Curabitur suscipit. Suspendisse quis nibh aliquam sem pulvinar sollicitudin. Etiam venenatis. Curabitur
   luctus.</p>
21
22             <!--This next element is 'commented-out' -->
23
24             <!--<p>Nunc venenatis lacus molestie sapien. Maecenas elementum aliquet velit. Ut eget mauris sed
    leo scelerisque lacinia. Nunc arcu magna, mollis id, ornare ac, pharetra sit amet, purus. Aliquam luctus
   consectetuer dolor.</p>-->
25
26         </section>
27
28     </body>
29
```

Above: Comments are invaluable: the more the merrier!

HOW TO USE CSS

Before delving any deeper into CSS we need to establish how to include it in an HTML document. There are two ways to do this.

EMBEDDED STYLE SHEETS

An **embedded** style sheet is one where all of the selectors and style rules appear in the `<head>` element of the HTML document they apply to. This is done by creating a `<style>` element (or elements, under some circumstances) within the page's `<head>` element.

```
5     <head>
6         <title>My Page</title>
7
8         <style>
9             body {
10                font-family:Arial, Helvetica, sans-serif;
11                font-size:14px;
12                color:black;
13            }
14            h1 {
15                font-size:24px;
16                font-weight:bold;
17            }
18            h2 {
19                font-size:18px;
20                font-weight:bold;
21                color:gray;
22            }
23            p {
24                margin-top:6px;
25                margin-bottom:6px
26            }
27        </style>
28
29     </head>
30
```

Above: Embedded style sheets are nested within the `<head>` of a document.

You then type the desired selectors and style rules inside this `<style>` element. This approach has the advantage of keeping all of the code for a page – HTML and CSS – within a single file, but can become difficult to manage for larger sites comprising many pages.

EXTERNAL STYLE SHEETS

With an **external** style sheet, the CSS code is written in a separate file and then linked to any HTML documents you wish to apply the style sheet to. A CSS document is simply a plain text file, typically saved with a '.css' filename extension.

Linking CSS Documents to HTML Documents

An external style sheet is associated with an HTML page using a <link> element placed in the <head> of the page:

```
<link type="text/css" rel="stylesheet"
href="myCssDocument.css" />.
```

Notice that the tag for this element is not paired with a closing tag, but includes a '/' before the final angle-bracket. This is commonly known as a self-closing tag or element; the reason it is self-closing is because no other elements can be nested within it.

```
4
5     <head>
6         <title>My Page</title>
7
8         <link rel="stylesheet" type="text/css" href="css/siteStyles.css" />
9
10    </head>
11
```

Above: External style sheets are associated with a web page via a <link> element.

There are a few attributes that need to be set: The `type` and `rel` attributes inform the browser what type of data to expect within the targeted document – always use the settings shown above. The `href` attribute defines the location and name of the CSS document itself. Typically this will be located on the same server as the web page, but often within a subfolder of the **site root**. Incidentally, the site root folder on most servers is called 'wwwroot'.

Hot Tip

A website consists of a hierarchy of files and folders, just like the hard disk in your computer. The top level of this hierarchy is known as the site root.

Below: CSS documents are often stored in a subfolder of the website's root folder.

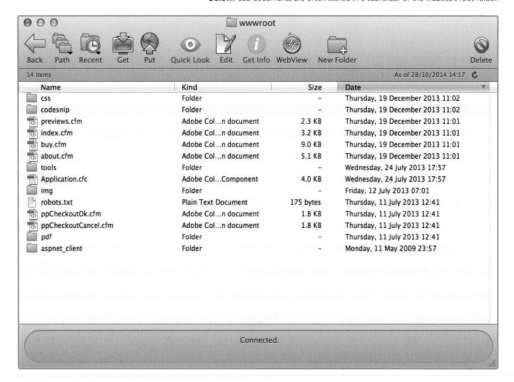

Advantages of External Style Sheets

External style sheets really come into their own when you are building a full website where it is normal for the pages that comprise the site to share a common look and feel. Because external style sheets can be linked to as many HTML pages as you like, they provide a central point from which you can modify and adapt the visual design of your entire site.

Above: External style sheets can be shared between multiple pages, perfect for common elements like headers.

MULTIPLE STYLE SHEETS

An HTML document can be linked to multiple style sheets. This allows you to arrange your selectors and style rules in logical groupings, with each group saved in a different CSS file. You then only need link a page to the style sheets that it needs.

It's also possible to mix embedded and external style sheets within the same document: style rules relating purely to the document can be embedded, and site-wide style rules can be derived from external style sheets.

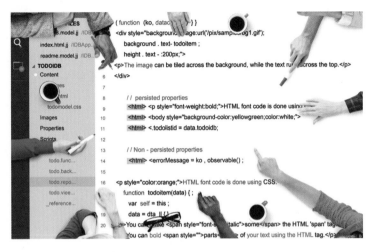

```
5   <head>
6       <title>My Page</title>
7
8       <link rel="stylesheet" type="text/css" href="css/siteStyles.css" />
9
10      <style>
11          body {
12              font-family:Arial, Helvetica, sans-serif;
13              font-size:14px;
14              color:black;
15          }
16          h1 {
17              font-size:24px;
18              font-weight:bold;
19          }
20          h2 {
21              font-size:18px;
22              font-weight:bold;
23              color:gray;
24          }
25          p {
26              margin-top:6px;
27              margin-bottom:6px
28          }
29      </style>
30
31  </head>
32
33  <body style="margin-left:20px; margin-right:20px">
34      |
35      <header>
36          <h1>A Page All About Me</h1>
37      </header>
```

Be aware that using multiple sheets increases the risk of applying conflicting values to a style property of an element, so if an element doesn't look as expected then it's worth digging around to check where the problematic style rule(s) is actually coming from.

Methods of Applying Styling

- **Inline**: A style rule is declared within an element's `style` attribute.

- **Embedded**: CSS code is written inside a `<style>` element in the `<head>` of an HTML document.

- **External**: CSS code is written inside a separate text file and associated with an HTML document via a `<link>` element.

Left: The three methods of applying CSS style rules to HTML elements.

NEW FEATURES OF HTML5

HTML5 is still HTML, but it is simply the latest version of the language. It contains many of the elements found in previous versions but also features a number of new elements and rules. In general, when somebody uses the term HTML5, they are referring to these new features.

SEMANTIC ELEMENTS

One of the aims of HTML5 is to introduce clear and consistent semantics into the language, such that the element names convey information about the purpose of an element and where it sits in the logical structure of a document.

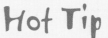

Hot Tip

Semantic elements are particularly helpful to the screenreader applications that assist with web browsing for people with visual impairment.

TUTORIALS   UPDATES   CONTRIBUTE   SLIDES   RESOURCES   SEARCH 🔍

HTML5 FEATURES
SEMANTICS

Semantics is one of the most distinctive features of the Web Platform versus other application platforms. Developers usually ignore or de-prioritize such feature but the mastery of it can bring many benefits to our projects.

The Web is text and text has a meaning. Ultimately the content that our browsers read is pure text. Web sites and web applications have been created in an ecosystem where text based content is linkable, searchable and mashable. In the open web scenario our content can be shown, fed and remixed by third parties, search engines and accessibility tools. All these benefits don't come for free. Automated tools can only do half of the job at recognizing the nature of the content. The better job the developer does at marking the right semantics of the content the easier will

be for the rest of the agents to deal with it. HTML5 provides a series of tools to make developers life easier too:

- New media elements.
- New structural elements.
- New semantics for internationalization.
- New link relation types.
- New attributes.
- New form types.
- New microdata syntax for additional semantics.

Tweet

Above: HTML5 places a lot of importance on semantics.

Therefore it includes a new set of elements that satisfies this need for semantic meaning, for example, `<header>`, `<video>`, `<article>` and `<footer>`. The fact that the element names convey exactly what these new elements are for is what makes them semantic.

Above: HTML5 works beautifully on mobile devices.

NEW FUNCTIONALITY

HTML5 introduced a lot of new functionality to web pages that would previously have required third-party plug-ins, such as Adobe Flash Player, to be installed on the end-user's browser. These new features are a breath of fresh air to developers because they make it infinitely simpler to add functionality, such as drag-and-drop, web forms, video, audio, 'live' graphics (including 3D), and much more.

Better for Mobile

Many popular browser plug-ins cannot be installed on mobile operating systems. HTML5 has fixed this by negating the need for many such third-party plug-ins, and so if you expect your web pages to be viewed on mobile devices then HTML5 is the only game in town.

WHAT IS CSS3?

CSS3 is still CSS; it is simply the latest version of the language. This third major version brings with it some important enhancements that make the language much more capable than previously.

VISUAL EFFECTS

One of the main advances in CSS3 is its ability to apply visual effects, such as drop shadow or blur, that would previously need to be produced in an image editor such as Adobe Photoshop. The effects on offer are fairly basic, but they are a godsend to developers who no longer have to jump back and forth between HTML editor and image editor just to put a little shadow on a graphic.

Below: A simple example of a CSS shadow.

Better Backgrounds

Another nifty CSS3 feature is `background-size`. This is a CSS property that allows background images (these being images that sit in the background of an HTML element) to automatically scale as required. By assigning a value to the property, such as `cover`, the image will fill an element's background: simple but effective.

Hot Tip

Just because you can do something doesn't mean you have to: too much eye candy can be as off-putting to visitors as too little.

Animations

The current big thing in CSS is animation. Previously, this was impossible in the browser without the help of third-party plug-ins or extensive scripting (or both), but now designers and developers can create slick and impressive animations with nothing more than CSS code. *See* page 106 for more on this.

Below: Check out this impressive CSS3 animation at http://codepen.io/juliangarnier/pen/idhuG

THE BENEFITS OF UNDERSTANDING HTML AND CSS

HTML and CSS are ubiquitous, and are used widely even outside of web development. As such, possessing an understanding of the languages can give you a considerable professional advantage.

BECOME THE EXPERT

Most companies nowadays have a web presence of some form or another, but many lack the in-house skills to support and maintain their sites properly. Possessing the ability to take on such a role, then, can make you an invaluable employee, especially in smaller businesses.

Below: An in-depth knowledge of CSS means better websites.

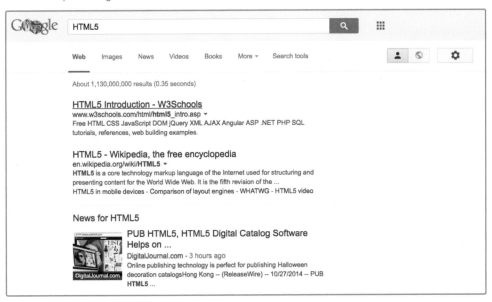

Ch-ch-ch-ch-ch Changes

As well as giving you the ability to problem-solve web pages, having a solid grounding in HTML and CSS provides you with the knowledge to make modifications to a site, confident that you will not break the site in the process.

Keeping up with the Trends

The graphical aspects of web design are heavily influenced by current vogues and trends. Having the ability to keep your site abreast of current fashions, then, ensures it always looks modern and fresh, helping you to build visitor numbers.

Faster Websites

The ability to recognize the right HTML and CSS for the right job can mean the difference between a slick and nimble experience for your visitors, or a slow and frustrating one... guess which they prefer!

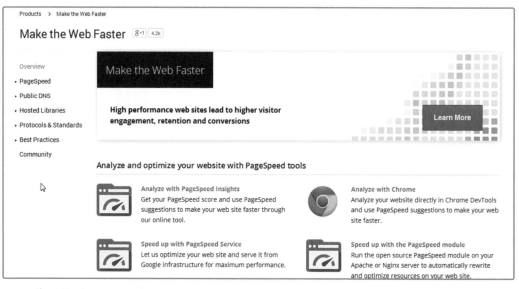

Above: Tweak your site to go faster to get more visitors.

What We've Learned

○ **HTML**: HyperText Markup Language; for constructing web pages.

○ **CSS**: Cascading Style Sheets; for styling web pages.

○ **Element**: The building block of HTML.

○ **Tag**: Demarks the start and end of an element.

○ **Attribute**: Provides the means to modify the behaviour and appearance of an element.

○ **Style property**: Assigns a value to a given CSS property.

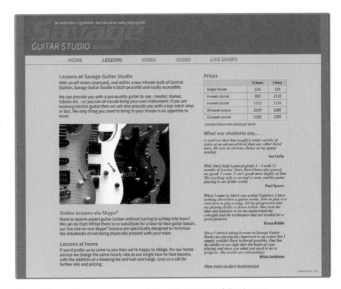

Above: The various components come together to give a full web page.

○ **Style rule**: A collection of style properties.

○ **Selector**: CSS component that specifies the HTML elements to which a style rule will be applied.

○ **Inline style**: A style rule attached to a single element via the element's `style` attribute.

○ **Embedded style sheet**: A set of style rules grouped by selector; located within a `<style>` element.

○ **External style sheet**: A set of style rules grouped by selector; located within a separate text document.

Homepage</title>

lor=white>

rder="0" cellpadding="10">

g src="images/logo.png">

>

Hello</h1>

>

DEMYSTIFYING HTML AND CSS

There is a baffling array of HTML elements and CSS properties that can be brought to bear on a website. Here we will demystify both with a deeper look into some of the essential HTML elements and CSS properties required for building vibrant and attractive websites.

THE BASIC BUILD

If you've been following along and paying attention, you should now know what a web page is, and have a basic understanding of its main building blocks. Now we're going to expand the picture a bit and consider websites. A website is a collection of HTML and CSS documents that are brought together to create a collection of useful content, displayed via an attractive user interface.

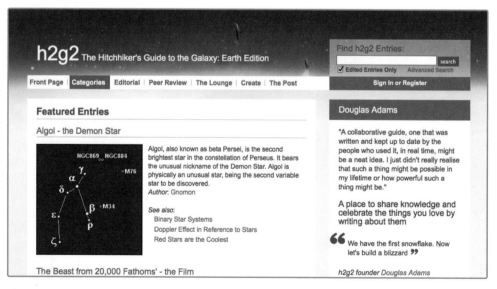

Above: Websites are made up of a number of pages.

Oodles of Elements

We've already discussed what an element is, but what we haven't mentioned is that there are hundreds of them! Don't fear though, you'll find that there is only a handful that you use or need on a regular basis; it is these elements that we'll be discussing over the coming pages.

Above: You can find a full list of elements and descriptions of what they do at http://www.quackit.com/html_5/tags/.

TALKING ABOUT HTML ELEMENTS

We discussed the `<html>`, `<head>` **and** `<body>` **elements in the previous chapter; these are the elements that should form the basic framework of all your web pages. Let's now look at the elements that go within this basic framework.**

A FLEXIBLE FRIEND

We're going to start by looking at a slightly unusual element: the `<div>`. What's unusual about it is that it has no specific intended use; it is essentially an empty container that you can use

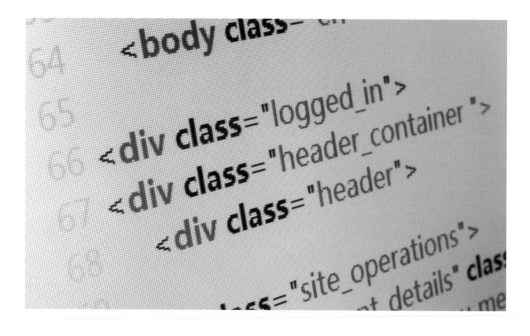

for a variety of purposes. One of the most common uses of a <div> is to allow you to group together sets of related elements, such as those that comprise the header of a page.

What's that, you say? You thought there was a <header> element in HTML5? Indeed there is, but there is no such thing in XHTML or older versions of HTML. So what did developers do prior to HTML5? To answer that we need to take a small detour...

The ID Attribute

You will recall that elements have attributes that can be assigned a value. One such attribute, available to all visual elements, is id. This allows you to provide a unique identifier for a specific element in your page, and is widely used in HTML. To see why, we need to look at what id means from the context of CSS.

```
 8
 9      <body>
10
11          <div>
12
13              <header>
14                  <h1>Divs are Containers</h1>
15              </header>
16
17              <div>
18                  <p>Divs can be nested within other divs</p>
19              </div>
20
21          </div>
22
23          <div>
24              <h2>Divs have no semantic meaning</h2>
25          </div>
26
27      </body>
28
```

Above: The <div> element is the developer's flexible friend.

```
11      <div id="main">
12
13              <header>
14                  <h1>Divs are Containers</h1>
15              </header>
16
17              <div id="contentBlock">
18                  <p>Divs can be nested within other divs</p>
19              </div>
20
21          </div>
22
23          <div id="divComment">
24              <h2>Divs have no semantic meaning</h2>
25          </div>
26
```

Above: The ID attribute gives an element a unique identifier.

Hot Tip

The value assigned to an element's id attribute must not be used as the id for any other element within the same page.

```
 6  body {
 7      position:relative;
 8      background-color:#FD5F12;
 9      margin:0px;
10      padding:0px;
11      width:100%;
12      height:100%;
13  }
14
15  #myElement {
16      position:fixed;|
17      width:1024px;
18      left:0px;
19      right:0px;
20      top:0px;
21      bottom:0px;
22      margin:0px auto 0px auto;
23      background-color:#D9D9D9;
24  }
25
```

Above: The ID selector allows a style rule to be targeted at a specific HTML element.

The ID Selector

An ID selector targets the single element whose id attribute value matches the ID selector. An ID selector looks like this:

#myElement {**style rule**}

The '#' (hash) states that this is an ID selector; its style rule will be applied to the HTML element whose id attribute value is "myElement".

What's All Of This Got To Do With <div>?

A <div> element's flexibility is delivered mainly via style properties, for it is these that determine how the <div> will be displayed on screen. So – finally getting back to the earlier question about the pre-HTML5 method of creating a header-like element – the answer is to write the following into the page's HTML:

<div id="header">**content**</div>

And add this to the page's CSS:

#header {**style rule**}

The Semantic Imperative

In HTML5, element names are intended to convey information about the element. For

example, a `<header>` element is intended to display information such as a company name, logo, and a navigation bar, and to be located at the top of the screen; this is self-evident, thanks to the name of the element.

The pre-HTML5 method of creating a page header, discussed above, is *valid* HTML5, but it's not *good* HTML5 because `<div>` conveys no meaning. Yes, an `id` value of `"header"` conveys meaning, but a developer could just as easily use a value of `"foobar"` – it would make no difference to the ID selector/attribute mechanism, but any semantic meaning would be lost. For this reason, browsers are not allowed to derive semantic meaning from `id` attributes.

Right: These three elements are valid HTML5 and will deliver identical results, but only one has semantic meaning.

```
8
9       <body>
10
11          <header>
12          </header>
13
14          <div id="header">
15          </div>
16
17          <div id="foobar">
18          </div>
19
20      </body>
21
```

```
 8
 9     <body>
10         <div id="wrapper">
11
12             <header>
13                 <!--Header content here-->
14             </header>
15
16             <section id="main">
17                 <!--Main page content here-->
18             </section>
19
20             <aside>
21                 <!--Aside content here-->
22             </aside>
23
24             <div id="adPanel">
25                 <!--Advertising content here-->
26             </div>
27
28             <footer>
29                 <div id="copyrightPanel">
30                     <!--Copyright boxout here-->
31                 </div>
32             </footer>
33
34         </div>
35     </body>
36
```

Above: `<div>` elements are unavoidable, but favour HTML5 semantic elements whenever possible.

The <div> Imperative

There are those who believe the `<div>` element should be retired because of its lack of a consistent and predictable semantic meaning. In reality the use of `<div>` is unavoidable because HTML5 cannot supply an element for every conceivable structural possibility. Best practice, then, is to only use `<div>` elements where there is no suitable HTML5 alternative. Let's take a look at those alternatives now...

WHAT'S A HEADER?

A `<header>` element is intended to sit at the top of a web page and typically will be the same across all of a site's pages. In general, a page's `<header>` will contain a logo and/or title of the page, and will often include the site navigation menu too.

Hot Tip

`<head>` **and** `<header>` **are separate and unrelated elements.**

WHAT'S A FOOTER?

The <footer> element should be positioned at the bottom of a web page, and is normally the same across all pages on a site. In general it is used for holding copyright information and additional navigation links, but it can contain any elements that you like.

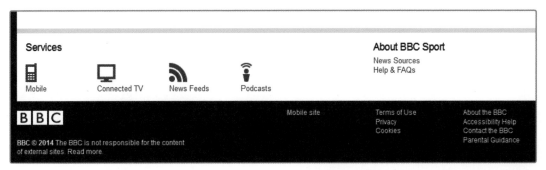

Above: The footer of a website is found at the bottom of the page.

WHAT'S CONTENT?

Content is the main bulk of information and media on your page: it's the stuff that your visitors have come to see! Unlike the <header> and <footer> elements that tend to be uniform throughout a site, the content area of a page will differ from page to page.

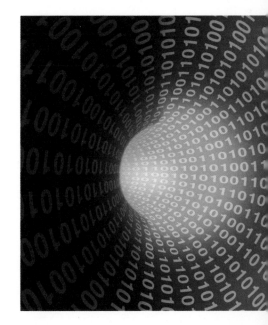

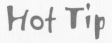

The menu/navigation system on a website is critical to how it works. Take a look at other websites to find one that works well for you and take inspiration from it.

```
1    <!DOCTYPE HTML>
2
3    <html>
4
5        <head>
6            <!--Head used for defining meta data about the page-->
7            <title>All Structural Elements</title>
8        </head>
9
10       <body>
11           <!--Body contains page's visual content-->
12
13           <header>
14               <!--Header content here; One header per page please-->
15               <nav>
16                   <!--Main page navigation control-->
17               </nav>
18           </header>
19
20           <section>
21               <!--A block of page content; Multiple sections allowed-->
22
23               <article>
24                   <!--Article content here; Multiple articles allowed-->
25               </article>
26
27           </section>
28
29           <footer>
30               <!--Footer content here; One footer per page please-->
31               <nav>
32                   <!--Footer navigation menu-->
33               </nav>
34           </footer>
35
36       </body>
37
38   </html>
39
```

Above: Structural elements provide a logical structure into which a page's content is written.

Page Sections

The <section> element is meant as a generic container for groups of related content, i.e. for 'sections' of your page. <section> elements typically follow the <header> element of a page.

OTHER STRUCTURAL ELEMENTS

The <header>, <section> and <footer> elements create both a page structure into which other elements can be placed, and a logical structure for the different types of information within a page. There are four more structural elements in HTML5 that you will use regularly.

Site Navigation

Most websites include a site navigation menu to allow users to move quickly and easily around the site; HTML5 provides the <nav> element to contain the elements of such a navigation menu. The <nav> element is generally created as a child of <header>, but this is not a requirement.

Article Element

The <article> element is intended as the final element in a structural chain in that it typically resides within another structural element such as <section>. The idea of <article> is that its content relates to a single subject, much like an article in a newspaper.

Aside Element

The idea behind an <aside> element is for it to display content that's related to content within another structural element, but that s not a direct part of that content. Semantically, any structural element can have a related <aside> element, but the typical usage is as a sidebar for showing things such as adverts, profile information, or links to other areas of the site.

Right: An <aside> element is intended for displaying content relating to <section> or <article> elements.

```
 9
10    <body>
11        <!--Body contains page's visual content-->
12
13        <header>
14            <!--Header content here; One header per page please-->
15            <nav>
16                <!--Main page navigation control-->
17            </nav>
18        </header>
19
20        <section>
21            <!--A block of page content; Multiple sections allowed-->
22
23            <article>
24                <!--Article content here; Multiple articles allowed-->
25            </article>
26
27            <aside>
28                <!--Aside content relates to other page content - here
29                it relates to the above article;
30                Multiple asides allowed-->
31            </aside>
32
33        </section>
34
35        <aside>
36            <!--Aside content here-->
37        </aside>
38
39        <footer>
40            <!--Footer content here; One footer per page please-->
41            <nav>
42                <!--Footer navigation menu-->
43            </nav>
44        </footer>
45
46    </body>
47
```

UNDERSTANDING CSS SELECTORS

We've already discussed CSS Type and ID selectors, but there is another important selector you need to know about: the Class selector. It is also possible to combine selectors in various ways; let's take a look.

```
127
128   .italic {
129        font-family:"source_sans_proitalic";
130   }
131
132   .bold {
133        font-family:"source_sans_probold";
134   }
135
136   .footerText {
137        position:absolute;
138        font:10px "source_sans_proregular";
139        color:#787878;
140        right:0px;
141        bottom:6px;
142        width:auto;
143        margin:6px 10px 6px auto;
144        padding:0px;
145   }
146
147   .navbarButton {
148        width:auto;
149        margin-left:4%;
150        margin-right:4%;
151        margin-top:9px;
152        padding:0px;
153        cursor:pointer;
154   }
155
156
157
```

CLASS SELECTORS

Recall that a Type selector targets any HTML elements of matching type, and that an ID selector targets the single HTML element with a matching id attribute value. A Class selector, then, allows you to target a specific *classification* of HTML elements. A Class selector is written like this (notice the '.' which precedes the class name):

.myClassName {**style rule**}

This selector would target any and all HTML elements that had been given the classification of myClassName .

Left: Class selectors target elements via the classification of those elements.

Typed Class Selectors

This can be taken a step further by combining a Class selector with a Type selector, for example, `article.newsStory {style rule}`. This selector would target all `<article>` elements that had been given a classification of `"newsStory"`. But how do we classify an element? Easy...

The Class Attribute

Every visual element has a `class` attribute. Here's how it looks: `<article class="newsStory">`. Once given a classification in this way, the element will receive the style rule associated with the `.newsStory` selector. If the selector had been `p.newsStory` then the above element would not have been selected because it is an `<article>`, not a `<p>`.

Hot Tip

Beware: Using Class selectors can increase the risk of conflicting style properties being applied to an element.

```
37
38      <body>
39          <header>
40              <h1>A Page All About Me</h1>
41              <nav class="navbarButton">Home | About Me | Contact</nav>
42          </header>
43
44          <section>
45              <h2 class="bold italic">What I'm thinking now</h2>
46              <p class="italic">Lorem ipsum dolor sit amet, consectetuer adipiscing elit. Sed sagittis ante
     malesuada velit. Curabitur suscipit. Suspendisse quis nibh aliquam sem pulvinar sollicitudin. Etiam venenatis.
     Curabitur luctus.</p>
47              <p>Nunc venenatis lacus molestie sapien. Maecenas elementum aliquet velit. Ut eget mauris sed leo
     scelerisque lacinia. Nunc arcu magna, mollis id, ornare ac, pharetra sit amet, purus. Aliquam luctus consectetuer
     dolor.</p>
48          </section>
49
50          <footer>
51              <p class="footerText">Cum sociis natoque penatibus et magnis dis parturient montes, nascetur
     ridiculus mus.</p>
52              <p class="footerText">Fusce libero nunc, tempor non, convallis ut, luctus sit amet, lectus.</p>
53          </footer>
54
55      </body>
56
```

Above: Elements can be given classifications via the `class` attribute.

Multiple Classifications

Imagine you have created three different Class selectors in a page's CSS: `.boldText`,
`.italicText` and `.underlinedText`, and assigned a suitable style rule to each, such as
`{font-weight:bold;}` etc. This would allow you to classify text-based elements using
these class names... but what if you want bold *and* italic text? Simple, just list the class names
in the element's `class` attribute, and separate each class name with a space.

```
2
3
4    <p class="boldText">Lorem ipsum dolor sit amet, consectetuer adipiscing elit.</p>
5    <p class="italicText">Sed sagittis ante malesuada velit.</p>
6    <p class="underlinedText">Curabitur suscipit. Suspendisse quis nibh aliquam sem.</p>
7    <p class="boldText italicText">Pulvinar sollicitudin. Etiam venenatis.</p>
8    <p class="boldText italicText underlinedText">Curabitur luctus.</p>
9
```

Above: An element's class attribute can accept a space-delimited list of class names. All will be applied.

COMPOUND SELECTORS

We've already mentioned one example of a compound selector, often known as a typed class selector, but there are many other ways of combining selectors; let's take a look at a few of them.

Multiple Type Selectors

If you want to create a style rule that will be applied to a number of different elements based on their element type, you can simply list those types in a selector and use a ',' to separate each type name. For example h2, h3, p {**style rule**} will target all <h2>, <h3> and <p> elements.

```
 2
 3
 4   h1, h2, h3 {
 5       font-family:"source_sans_probold";
 6       font-weight:bold;
 7   }
 8
 9   article h2 {
10       color:blue;
11   }
12
13   article p {
14       font-family:"source_sans_regular";
15   }
16
17   nav > p {
18       colour:red;
19       cursor:pointer;
20   }
```

Descendant Selectors

There are times when we want to target an element based upon its position within the nested structure of the HTML. For example, we may want to target all <p> elements that are descended from (i.e. nested within, at any level) an <article> element: article p {**style rule**} (notice the space between the type names in the selector).

Left: CSS has numerous forms of selector.

Child Selectors

A child selector targets elements that are a child of another element (note that a Descendant selector also targets grandchildren, great grandchildren, etc.). So a selector of `article > h3 {style rule}` would target all <h3> elements that were direct children of an <article> element (notice the '>' between the type names in the selector).

A LOT TO LEARN

CSS is a simple language, but the devil is in the detail – and there's a *lot* of detail, much more than we can cover here. If you want to find out more then check out some of the many great websites and books dedicated to the subject.

Above: There are many sites dedicated to the subject of CSS.

TEXT-BASED ELEMENTS

Most web pages contain text – often quite a lot of it – and so unsurprisingly there is a collection of elements that are dedicated to displaying text. Text elements tend to be nested within the structural elements that we've discussed previously.

HEADING TEXT

There is a group of HTML elements that is dedicated to displaying headings; their names are very easy to remember. The first is called <h1>, the second <h2> and so on until we reach <h6> .

Hot Tip

<h4> **to** <h6> **are rarely used – just how many levels of heading does one need?!**

```
 8
 9      <body>
10
11          <h1>Heading level 1</h1>
12          <h2>Heading level 2</h2>
13          <h3>Heading level 3</h3>
14          <h4>Heading level 4</h4>
15          <h5>Heading level 5</h5>
16          <h6>Heading level 6</h6>
17
18      </body>
19
```

Above: There are six levels of heading element in HTML.

Heading Levels

The number in the heading element's name represents the 'level' of the heading, in other words how important (and therefore prominent) the heading is. <h1> is the most prominent, and <h6> the least.

Heading Semantics

Prior to HTML5 the different levels of heading represented nothing more than different degrees of visual prominence: <h1> the boldest and largest, <h6> the smallest and lightest. HTML5 goes a step further and imposes semantic meaning on the different heading levels.

Heading level 1

Heading level 2

Heading level 3

Heading level 4

Heading level 5

Heading level 6

Above: <h1> is the most prominent heading, <h6> the least.

The easiest way to explain this is by using the analogy of a book such as the one you are reading now. If a web page were a chapter in a book, then <h1> would be analogous to the chapter title, so <h1> should only appear once in a web page.

<h2> would be analogous to section headings within a chapter, and so can appear more than once after an <h1>. <h3> is analogous to subheadings within a section... and so on. Heading semantics can be tricky, but keep the book analogy in mind – it helps!

Logical Structure of Headings

The semantic nature of HTML5 headings means that they also infer a logical structure. Returning to our book analogy, the parent of a subheading (<h3>) will be a section heading (<h2>), and the parent of a section heading will be a chapter heading (<h1>). But what if you want to create a single heading that has two components: a 'stand-first' and 'tagline', so to speak?

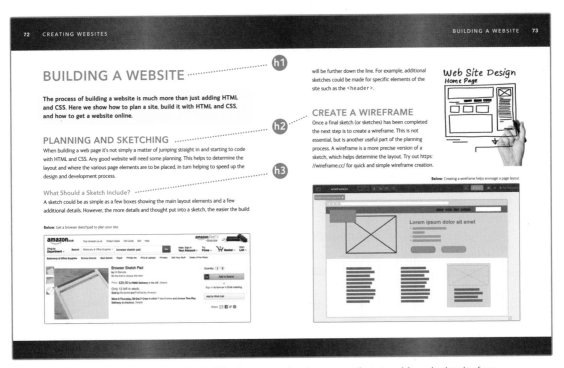

Above: Like the levels of heading in a book, HTML5 headings impart a logical structure on the text, so <h1> can be thought of as a chapter heading, <h2> can be thought of as a section heading and <h3> can be thought of as a sub-section heading.

Heading Groups

We might create a two-part heading like this:

```
<h1>HTML and CSS</h1>
<h2>The Language of the Internet</h2>
```

Unfortunately there's a problem here: the `<h2>` is a subheading of `<h1>`, but as things stand it's denoting a new section in the logical structure of the page. The solution is the `<hgroup>` element; it allows you to group together multiple levels of heading without implying that you are creating new sections in the logical structure – the first heading in the `<hgroup>` is the heading-level that will be inferred. So instead of the above we would write this:

```
<hgroup>
    <h1>HTML and CSS</h1>
    <h2>The Language of the Internet</h2>
</hgroup>
```

Now, the `<h2>` element will be considered part of the `<h1>`, and semantic wellbeing is restored.

```
11
12          <!--Semantically incorrect...:-->
13          <h1>HTML and CSS</h1>
14          <h2>The Language of the Internet</h2>
15
16          <!--Semantically correct...:-->
17          <hgroup>
18              <h1>HTML and CSS</h1>
19              <h2>The Language of the Internet</h2>
20          </hgroup>
21
```

Above: An `<hgroup>` element assists in maintaining semantic accuracy in headings.

PARAGRAPH TEXT

You'll be pleased to know that paragraph text (the main body text of a page) is much simpler than headings. We have just one paragraph element, <p>. Generally a <p> contains only text, but it can also have images and certain other elements embedded within it.

Styling Paragraphs

A common strategy for styling paragraphs is to create a p Type selector in which to define the very basic aspects of your paragraph style, such as the font, and then create a collection of Class selectors that apply specific styling, such as bold text, underlining and italics. You can then assign the desired class name(s) to a given <p> element as required.

```
7
8          <style>
9
10             .boldText {
11                 font-weight:bold;
12             }
13
14             .italicText {
15                 font-style:italic;
16             }
17
18             .underlinedText {
19                 text-decoration:underline;
20             }
21
22         </style>
23
```

```
25
26     <body>
27
28         <p class="boldText">Lorem ipsum dolor sit amet, consectetuer adipiscing elit.</p>
29         <p class="italicText">Sed sagittis ante malesuada velit.</p>
30         <p class="underlinedText">Curabitur suscipit. Suspendisse quis nibh aliquam sem.</p>
31         <p class="boldText italicText">Pulvinar sollicitudin. Etiam venenatis.</p>
32         <p class="boldText italicText underlinedText">Curabitur luctus.</p>
33
34     </body>
35
```

Above: Creating a number of Class selectors containing simple rules makes for easy paragraph styling.

Styling Within a Paragraph

There are many occasions when you will want to change the text format within a paragraph, such as when you wish to emphasize a word or passage with *italic* or **bold** text. There are a few ways to do this: italicizing can be achieved by wrapping a span of text in an <em> (emphasis) element:

```
<p>Mary had a <em>little</em> lamb</p>
```

Or for bold text:

```
<p>It really <b>was</b> a dear</p>
```

A better way, however, is to use the <span> element. It is much more flexible because rather than giving a single style property change, it can apply a whole style rule – or rules – in one go:

> ### Hot Tip
>
> **When adding child elements to a text-based element it is normal to place the new tags within the text without creating new lines or indentation in the code.**

```
<p>But she <span class="redText italic">couldn't tell the
difference</span></p>
```

Mary had a *little* lamb

It really **was** a dear

But she *couldn't tell the difference*

Above: Text format changes within a paragraph are easy with the <span> element.

HYPERLINKS

A website would not be a website if it didn't have hyperlinks. They are the mechanism that allow web browsing to happen at all, and without them there would be no way to navigate within a site, or to direct people to external sites. A website would be nothing more than a single page!

THE ANCHOR ELEMENT

At the heart of the hyperlink mechanism lies the anchor element, < a >. It is called this because one of its uses is for marking specific points in a page. This use remains, but < a > is most commonly used for creating hyperlinks.

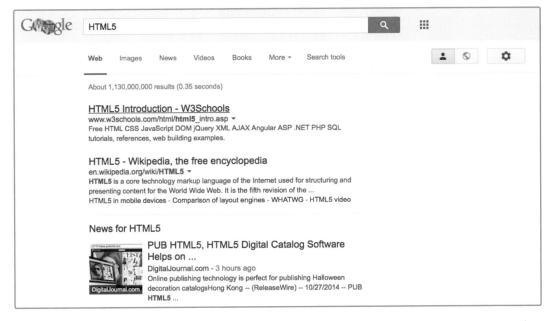

Above: Without hyperlinks there'd be no such thing as Google.

```
8
9
10      <body>
11
12          <p>HTML5 info can be found on <a href="www.google.com">Google</a>. It's a useful resource.</p>
13
14      </body>
15
16
```

Above: Using an <a> element to create a hyperlink.

Creating a Hyperlink

We create a hyperlink by wrapping an <a> element around the text we want to convert into a hyperlink – the **URL** (or web address) that you want to link to is defined in the href attribute of the <a>.

URLs

URL stands for Uniform Resource Locator. There are two common forms of URL: **absolute** and **relative**. The former defines a full web address for a resource, starting with 'http://'. The latter operates relative to the current file, and can only address resources within the same site as that file. A relative URL states the path from the current page to a resource, along with the resource's filename, and looks like 'pathToFile/filename'.

STYLING LINKS

As with all elements, <a> has a default appearance derived ultimately from the browser's default style sheet. In the case of <a> that default styling is typically for blue underlined text. We can override this, of course, by attaching style rules to an <a> element, either directly or via style inheritance.

However, a hyperlink typically changes styling depending upon its state, i.e. if the mouse pointer is over it, if the user has previously clicked the link, etc. This state-based styling is achieved through CSS **Pseudo-Class** selectors.

Hot Tip

A web browser provides a default style sheet. This defines values for all CSS properties, and is the starting point of the style cascade.

Below: Hyperlinks have a default appearance.

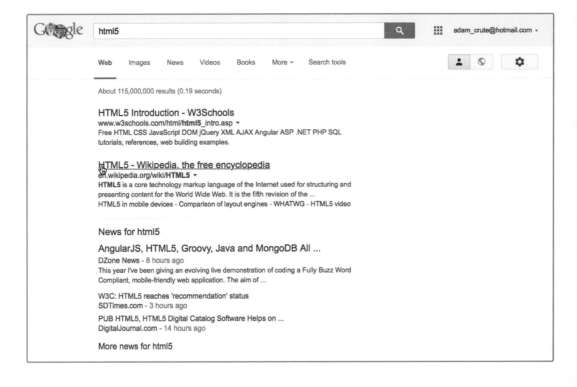

Pseudo-Class Selectors

A pseudo-class is a class that's not specifically declared in an HTML document, but that becomes available when the page is being viewed in a browser. There are a few different ones, but with hyperlinks the pseudo-classes we're concerned with are :link (the base-state of a hyperlink), :hover (the mouse pointer is over the hyperlink) and :visited (the hyperlink has been clicked). In CSS we use these pseudo-class selectors as a suffix to another selector.

```
1
2  a:link {
3      color:blue;
4  }
5
6  a:hover {
7      color:red;
8      text-decoration:none;
9  }
10
11 a:visited {
12     color:purple;
13 }
14
15 .navButton:hover {
16     colour:blue;
17     background-color:gray;
18     cursor:pointer;
19 }
20
21 #headerLogo:hover {
22     border-color:blue;
23     border-style:solid;
24     border-width:2px;
25     cursor:pointer;
26 }
```

Above: Pseudo-Class selectors are added as a suffix to another selector.

OPENING A HYPERLINK IN A NEW WINDOW

It's often desirable to open a hyperlink in a new browser window so your own site remains open in the background. This is done via the target attribute of the <a> element, like so:

```
<a href="http://www.bbc.co.uk" target="_blank">
```

LISTS

Lists are a staple part of web design. There are two basic list types, unordered and ordered, both of which will contain one or more list items. A third type, the definition list, creates a glossary-like structure of titles and associated information.

LIST ITEMS

Before looking at the list elements themselves, let's consider what goes into a list. In HTML this is a **list item** element, `<li>`. Typically, these contain text but, as with other text-based elements, can also contain other elements such as images and hyperlinks. <li> elements are rendered in the order in which they appear in the parent list element.

Above: Lists allow us to present information in an attractive and logical manner.

Unordered List

- HTML5 is largely made up of elements.
- Elements are demarked by opening and closing tags.
- Attributes allow you to modify an element.

Ordered List

1. HTML5 is largely made up of elements.
2. Elements are demarked by opening and closing tags.
3. Attributes allow you to modify an element.

Definition List

HTML5
    is largely made up of elements.
Elements
    are demarked by opening and closing tags
Attributes
    allow you to modify an element.

UNORDERED LISTS

An unordered list, `<ul>`, is a simple bullet-point list. Each `<li>` added to the list creates a new bullet-point. The `list-style-type` and `list-style-image` style properties determine the appearance of the bullet-point markers.

Hot Tip

It is common to place a `<ul>` within a page's `<nav>` element in order to create a navigation menu. The `<ul>` can be styled to render its items horizontally or vertically.

```
13
14              ul {
15                  list-style-type:circle;
16              }
17
18              ol {
19 ▼                list-style-type:decimal;
20              }                          ● armenian
21          </style>                       ● circle
22      </head>                            ● cjk-ideographic
23                                         ● decimal
24      <body>                             ● decimal-leading-zero
25                                         ● disc
26          <h2>Unordered List</h2>        ● georgian
27          <ul>                           ● hebrew
28              <li>HTML5 is largely made  ● hiragana
                 up of elements.</li>      ● hiragana-iroha
29              <li>Elements are demarked by opening and closing tags.</li>
30              <li>Attributes allow you to modify an element.</li>
31          </ul>
32
33          <h2>Ordered List</h2>
34          <ol>
35              <li>HTML5 is largely made up of elements.</li>
36              <li>Elements are demarked by opening and closing tags.</li>
37              <li>Attributes allow you to modify an element.</li>
38          </ol>
39
40      </body>
41
```

Above: `<ul>` and `<ol>` lists only differ in the way each item is marked.

ORDERED LISTS

In an ordered list, `<ol>`, each item is marked with a sequential number or letter. Interestingly, the style of numbering is determined by the `list-style-type` style property, the same as with a `<ul>`. This shows that the only real difference between `<ul>` and `<ol>` is the styling!

DEFINITION LISTS

A definition list, `<dl>`, is a bit like a glossary: each item consists of a title and a block of information relating to the title. This means that each item in the list actually has two components: a `<dt>` element for the title and a `<dd>` element for the information (the second 'd' representing the word 'data').

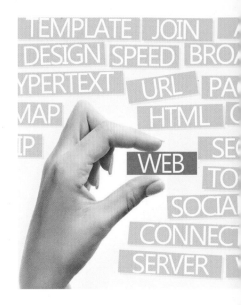

```
19    <body>
20
21        <h2>Definition List</h2>
22        <dl>
23            <dt>HTML5</dt>
24            <dd>is largely made up of elements.</dd>
25            <dt>Elements</dt>
26            <dd>are demarked by opening and closing tags</dd>
27            <dt>Attributes</dt>
28            <dd>allow you to modify an element.</dd>
29        </dl>
30
31    </body>
32
```

Definition List

HTML5
  is largely made up of elements.
Elements
  are demarked by opening and closing tags
Attributes
  allow you to modify an element.

Above: Each item in a `<dl>` comprises two elements: `<dt>` and `<dd>`.

LISTS WITHIN LISTS

If you wish to create a multi-tiered list, the solution is to place a new list element within an `<li>` or `<dd>` element. You can do this with any of the three list types, and you can mix and match the different types as required.

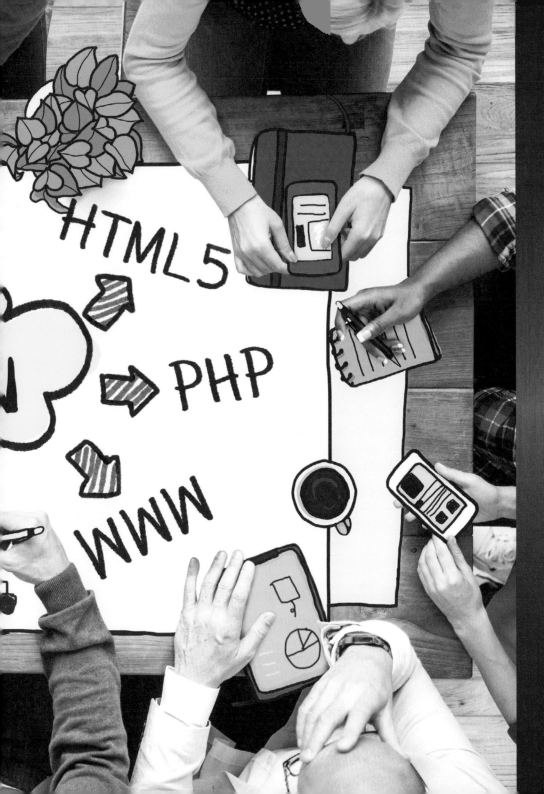

CREATING WEBSITES

BUILDING A WEBSITE

The process of building a website is much more than just adding HTML and CSS. Here we show how to plan a site, build it with HTML and CSS, and how to get a website online.

PLANNING AND SKETCHING

When building a web page it's not simply a matter of jumping straight in and starting to code with HTML and CSS. Any good website will need some planning. This helps to determine the layout and where the various page elements are to be placed, in turn helping to speed up the design and development process.

What Should a Sketch Include?

A sketch could be as simple as a few boxes showing the main layout elements and a few additional details. However, the more details and thought put into a sketch, the easier the build

Below: Get a browser sketchpad to plan your site.

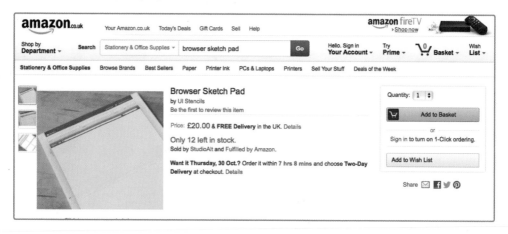

will be further down the line. For example, additional sketches could be made for specific elements of the site such as the `<header>`.

CREATE A WIREFRAME

Once a final sketch (or sketches) has been completed the next step is to create a wireframe. This is not essential, but is another useful part of the planning process. A wireframe is a more precise version of a sketch, which helps determine the layout. Try out https://wireframe.cc/ for quick and simple wireframe creation.

Below: Creating a wireframe helps envisage a page layout.

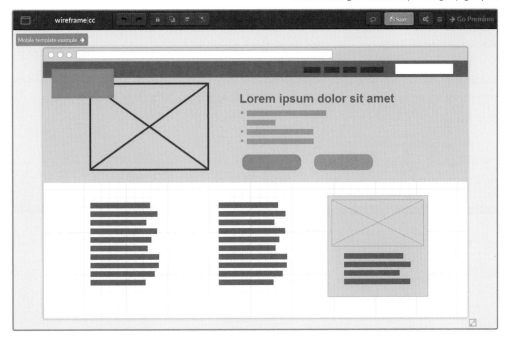

TOOLS OF THE TRADE

You cannot build a website without the right tools. The basic set-up includes a text editor and an image editor. The text editor will be where the HTML and CSS is created, while the image editor will allow for the manipulation and modification of images and graphics.

Hot Tip

If you are using TextEdit on a Mac, be sure to switch to plain text mode before you start coding: [shift]+[cmd]+[T].

TEXT EDITORS

Windows and MacOSX both come with text editors: Notepad and TextEdit respectively. These are ideal for beginners, but are very basic. There are some free editors worth checking out. Try Notepad++ (http://notepad-plus-plus.org); Brackets (http://brackets.io); CoffeeCup Free HTML Editor (http://www.coffeecup.com/free-editor/) or the more advanced Sublime Text (http://www.sublimetext.com)

TopStyle 5, a powerful HTML5 & CSS3 editor for Windows.

What makes TopStyle 5 special ▶
What's new in TopStyle 5?
Download and try it free!

Above: Try different text editors to see which one works for you.

HTML EDITORS

HTML editors provide lots of features for the web developer. The best known is Adobe Dreamweaver; it is excellent but is expensive and can only be licensed on a subscription basis. HTML editors offer features such as code-hinting and code-colouring, both of which are invaluable to the developer.

```
 3   <html>
 4
 5       <head>
 6           <!--TO DO: Come up with a better title for the page -->
 7           <title>My Page</title>
 8           <link rel="stylesheet" type="text/css" href="siteStyles.css"/>
 9           <style>
10               body {
11                   font-family:Arial, Helvetica, sans-serif;
12                   font-size:14px;
13                   color:black;
14                   padd:
15               }              ● padding
16       </style>             ● padding-bottom
17   </head>                  ● padding-left
18                            ● padding-right
19   <body>                   ● padding-top
20       <header>
21           <h1>A Page All About Me</h1>
22       </header>
23
24       <section>
25           <h2>What I'm thinking now</h2>
26           <!-- Placeholder text...-->
27           <p>Lorem ipsum dolor sit amet, consectetuer adipiscing <a href="contactPage.html">elit</a>.
Sed sagittis ante malesuada velit. Curabitur suscipit. Suspendisse quis nibh aliquam sem pulvinar
sollicitudin. Etiam venenatis. Curabitur luctus.</p>
28       </section>
29
```

Code-hinting saves you from having to remember every element and style property name.

Code-colouring helps the developer recognize types of code. Notice how elements, attributes, CSS, comments and plain text content are all easily distinguishable.

Line numbering helps you to know where you are in the document especially if you need to move back and forth through the document.

IMAGE EDITORS

You will often find yourself needing to edit images and create graphics for your site. The professional choice is a combination of Adobe's Photoshop and Illustrator, but this is an expensive route to take with a steep learning curve.

Image and Graphics Editor Links

- **PaintShop Pro (Win)**: www.paintshoppro.com
- **CorelDRAW (Win)**: www.coreldraw.com
- **Pixelmator (Mac)**: www.pixelmator.com
- **iDraw (Mac)**: www.indeeo.com
- **Adobe Photoshop (Win/Mac)**: www.adobe.com
- **Adobe Illustrator (Win/Mac)**: www.adobe.com

BUILDING A WEB PAGE

We've covered a lot of theory and information over the preceding chapters, so let's start putting it into practice. The first step is to create an HTML document and add the basic structure of elements that we're going to use.

CREATE A WORKING FOLDER

The first thing to do is to create a folder in which to store all of the files for our page. Your Documents folder would be a good place for this or, better still, create a folder called MySites inside your Home folder; this can then be a central location for all of the sites you develop. Wherever you put it, the folder you create for an individual site should have the same name as the site. Let's call this one MyFirstSite.

Hot Tip

Don't use spaces in file or folder names. Either remove the spaces and capitalize each word (known as CamelCase), or replace the spaces with underscores or hyphens.

Above: All files for a site should be stored in a single outer folder. It's also handy to place all of your sites into a single outer folder.

Create a Basic Structure

1. Create a new page in your editor of choice and add the DOCTYPE declaration at the very top of the page.

```
1  <!DOCTYPE HTML>
2
3  <html>
4
5      <head>
6
7      </head>
8
9      <body>
10
11     </body>
12
```
Step 2: Start with the essential elements.

2. Add the base elements `<html>`, `<head>` and `<body>`, and save the page as 'index.html' inside your MyFirstSite folder.

```
1  <!DOCTYPE HTML>
2
3  <html>
4
5      <head>
6          <title>My First Web Page</title>
7      </head>
8
9      <body>
10
11     </body>
12
13 </html>
14
```
Step 3: Choose a title for your page wisely; it can make the difference between the page getting visitors or not.

3. Now add a `<title>` element as a child of (i.e. within) the `<head>` element. Make the title relevant as this will show up in search-engine listings.

4. Now we'll create the basic layout structure for the visible content of the page. Add `<header>`, `<section>` and `<footer>` elements as children of the `<body>` element.

> ## Hot Tip
> The default page of any website – the one that is loaded if no specific page is requested – is most often called index.html. There are other names that work, but this one is best.

```
1  <!DOCTYPE HTML>
2
3  <html>
4
5      <head>
6          <title>My First Web Page</title>
7      </head>
8
9      <body>
10
11         <header>
12         </header>
13
14         <section>
15         </section>
16
17         <footer>
18         </footer>
19
20     </body>
21
22 </html>
23
```
Step 4: Add the elements that make up the basic page structure.

```
 1  <!DOCTYPE HTML>
 2
 3  <html>
 4
 5      <head>
 6          <title>My First Web Page</title>
 7      </head>
 8
 9      <body>
10
11          <header>
12              <nav>Home | About | Contact </nav>
13          </header>
14
15          <section>
16          </section>
17
18          <footer>
19          </footer>
20
21      </body>
22
```

Step 5: Create a <nav> element inside the <header>.

```
 1  <!DOCTYPE HTML>
 2
 3  <html>
 4
 5      <head>
 6          <title>My First Web Page</title>
 7      </head>
 8
 9      <body>
10
11          <header>
12              <nav>Home | About | Contact </nav>
13              <hgroup>
14                  <h1>My First Web Page</h1>
15                  <h2>It may be basic, but it rocks</h2>
16              </hgroup>
17          </header>
18
19          <section>
20          </section>
21
22          <footer>
23          </footer>
24
25      </body>
26
```

Step 6: Place the heading elements inside the <header>, and then add some suitable text.

5. We need a means of navigating our site, so add a <nav> element as the first child of the <header>, and enter some titles for pages you're likely to include in your site.

6. Now we are going to add some text headings to the <header> element of the page. These headings will be related, so we'll create them inside an <hgroup> element.

7. The main content of the page is going to be placed inside the <section> element. In the next chapter we're going to add an image that represents the site's content (*see* page 95), but for now we'll keep to just text.

```
16                </hgroup>
17            </header>
18
19            <section>
20                <h2>Welcome To My World!</h2>
21                <p>Lorem ipsum dolor sit amet, consectetuer adipi
velit. Curabitur suscipit.</p>
22                <p>Suspendisse quis nibh aliquam sem pulvinar sol
luctus. Nunc venenatis lacus molestie sapien.</p>
23                <p>Maecenas elementum aliquet velit!</p>
24            </section>
25
26            <footer>
27            </footer>
28
29        </body>
```

Step 8: Add multiple <p> elements to make the text easy to read.

8. We're going to add some text to accompany the image we'll be adding later. Use an <h2> heading for this because <h1> has been used in our <header>. Then use <p> elements under the <h2> to hold some introductory text.

Hot Tip

From the point of view of heading semantics, an <hgroup> makes all headings embedded within it act as a single heading of the type first declared in the <hgroup>.

9. The <aside> element typically contains content that relates to the main content of a page. Add an <aside> after the <section> element, and add some content to it.

```
19            <section>
20                <h2>Welcome To My World!</h2>
21                <p>Lorem ipsum dolor sit amet, consectetuer adipiscing elit. Sed sagittis ante malesuada
velit. Curabitur suscipit.</p>
22                <p>Suspendisse quis nibh aliquam sem pulvinar sollicitudin. Etiam venenatis. Curabitur
luctus. Nunc venenatis lacus molestie sapien.</p>
23                <p>Maecenas elementum aliquet velit!</p>
24            </section>
25
26            <aside>
27                <h3>By the way...</h3>
28                <p>Ut eget mauris sed leo scelerisque lacinia. Nunc arcu magna, mollis id, ornare ac,
pharetra sit amet, purus.</p>
29                <p>Aliquam luctus consectetuer dolor? In placerat, diam et suscipit posuere, lacus orci
vestibulum libero, vulputate faucibus felis leo sit amet elit: Sed hendrerit felis non urna.</p>
30            </aside>
31
32            <footer>
33            </footer>
```

Step 9: Add a <h3> element followed by a few <p> elements. Place them all within an <aside> element.

10. Finally, we'll add some content to the `<footer>`. This can be information such as contact details, address and copyright information.

```
27              <h3>By the way...</h3>
28              <p>Ut eget mauris sed leo scelerisque lacinia. Nunc arcu magna, mollis id,
29              <p>Aliquam luctus consectetuer dolor? In placerat, diam et suscipit posuere
30          </aside>
31
32          <footer>
33              <p>Donec interdum dui at est. Pellentesque sit amet urna</p>
34              <p>(C) J. Smith, 2014</p>
35              <p><a href="mailto:jsmith789@somehost.com">jsmith789@somehost.com</a></p>
36          </footer>
37
38      </body>
```

Step 10: Make sure the info in your `<footer>` is useful.

11. To complete the `<footer>`, add the same navigation menu that we used at the top of the page; simply copy the whole `<nav>` element and paste it as the last child of the <footer> element.

```
26          <aside>
27              <h3>By the way...</h3>
28              <p>Ut eget mauris sed leo scelerisque lacinia. Nunc arcu magna, mollis id,
29              <p>Aliquam luctus consectetuer dolor? In placerat, diam et suscipit posuere
30          </aside>
31
32          <footer>
33              <p>Donec interdum dui at est. Pellentesque sit amet urna</p>
34              <p>(C) J. Smith, 2014</p>
35              <p><a href="mailto:jsmith789@somehost.com">jsmith789@somehost.com</a></p>
36              <nav>Home | About | Contact </nav>
37          </footer>
38
39      </body>
40
41  </html>
42
43
44
```

Step 11: Adding a navigation menu to the bottom of the screen can prove useful.

12. Save your work. Now find the file on your computer and launch it in your web browser to take a look. Rather basic perhaps, but we haven't cracked out the CSS yet...

Step 12: It may be basic, but it's all your own work. Well done.

STYLING A PAGE WITH CSS

The HTML for our page is now in place but it looks fairly basic as things stand. Let's deal with that now by adding some CSS styling to the page.

EMBEDDED OR EXTERNAL?

The first choice is whether to add the CSS as an embedded or external style sheet. Given that our site only has a single page (for now at least) we'll use an embedded sheet so that all of the code for the page is in one location.

Creating the CSS Code

1. Open index.html in your editor if it isn't already open, and then add a `<style>` element inside the `<head>`.

```
1   <!DOCTYPE HTML>
2
3   <html>
4
5      <head>
6          <title>My First Web Page</title>
7          <style>
8          </style>
9      </head>
10
11     <body>
12
```

Step 1: Add an embedded style sheet in the `<head>` of the page.

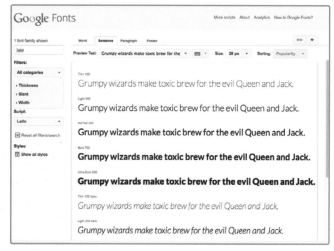

Hot Tip

Web fonts allow you to use fonts on your site that aren't installed on your visitors' computers.

Step 2: Choose a font to use on your website.

2. Now we need a font for our text. There is a limited set of web standard fonts that are installed on all computers; using one of these is an option. The better option is to use a web font: head over to Google Fonts (www.google.com/fonts) and find a font you like, preferably one with a lot of variations, such a Lato.

3. Click the Quick-Use button and select a font variation. You will now be shown a block of code for a `<link>` element. Copy it and paste it into the `<head>` of your page, before the `<style>` element.

Step 3: Copy the `<link>` element code from Google Fonts.

```
Standard    @import    Javascript

3. Add this code to your website:

<link href='http://fonts.googleapis.com/css?family=Lato:400,700,400italic' rel='styleshe
```

```
 3   <html>
 4
 5       <head>
 6           <title>My First Web Page</title>
 7           <link rel='stylesheet' type='text/css' href='http://fonts.googleapis.com/css?family=Lato:400,700,400italic'/>
 8           <style>
 9               body {
10                   font-family:"Lato";
11               }
12           </style>
13       </head>
14
15       <body>
16
17           <div id="wrapper">
18               <header>
19                   <nav>Home | About | Contact </nav>
20                   <hgroup>
21                       <h1>My First Web Page</h1>
22                       <h2>It may be basic, but it rocks</h2>
23                   </hgroup>
24               </header>
25
26               <section>
```

Steps 4 and 5: Use the `font-family` style property to define a font within a style rule, and wrap the page's content in a `<div>`.

4. To make this the default font for the entire page we create a `body` Type selector and set the `font-family` property within its style rule.

5. In order to be able to centralize the page's content area within the browser window, we're going to wrap all of that content in a `<div>` element. Assign an `id` attribute value of `"wrapper"` to the `<div>`.

```
 8           <style>
 9
10               body {
11                   font-family:"Lato";
12                   font-size:14px;
13               }
14
15               #wrapper {
16                   width:1000px;
17                   height:auto;
18                   margin-left:auto;
19                   margin-right:auto;
20               }
21
22           </style>
23
```

6. We can now style the wrapper `<div>` by using a CSS ID selector of `#wrapper`. Add the code in the screenshot to make the site 1000 pixels wide and centred in the browser window.

Step 6: Styling the wrapper allows it to be centralized in the browser window.

```
8          <style>
9
10             body {
11                 font-family:"Lato";
12                 font-size:14px;
13             }
14
15             #wrapper {
16                 width:1000px;
17                 height:auto;
18                 margin-left:auto;
19                 margin-right:auto;
20             }
21
22             section {
23                 width:700px;
24                 height:auto;
25                 float:left;
26             }
27
28         </style>
29
```

```
11                 font-size:14px;
12             }
13
14             #wrapper {
15                 width:1000px;
16                 height:auto;
17                 margin-left:auto;
18                 margin-right:auto;
19             }
20
21             section {
22                 width:700px;
23                 height:auto;
24                 float:left;
25             }
26
27             aside {
28                 width:300px;
29                 float:right;
30             }
31
32         </style>
```

Step 7: Content within the wrapper now positions itself relative to the wrapper rather than the browser window.

7. The `<section>` element in our page contains the main page content. Copy the CSS code in the screenshot to make it 700 pixels wide and positioned to the left of the wrapper.

Hot Tip

Try using more than one font on a website: one for headings, and one for paragraph text. Best practice is to use no more than three fonts on a page.

8. Now we'll make the `<aside>` element 300 pixels wide and make it float to the left of the `<section>` element. The widths of section and aside will now add up to the 1000 pixel width of the wrapper `<div>`.

Step 8: Floating is a method of positioning one element alongside another.

Step 9: Size the `<footer>` to be the same width as the content above it – this ensures it will float below that content.

```
22          section {
23              width:700px;
24              height:auto;
25              float:left;
26          }
27
28          aside {
29              width:300px;
30              float:right;
31          }
32
33          footer {
34              width:1000px;
35              height:auto;
36              float:left:
37          }
```

Step 10: Style heading elements such that they have reducing levels of visual prominence.

```
40          h1 {
41              font-weight:bold;
42              font-size:26px;
43              color:#990000;
44          }
45
46          h2 {
47              font-weight:bold;
48              font-size:22px;
49              color:#CC6600;
50          }
51
52          h3 {
53              font-weight:normal;
54              font-size:18px;
55              font-style:italic;
56              color:#FF9933;
57          }
58
59          hgroup > h1 {
60              margin-bottom:3px;
61          }
62
63          hgroup > h2 {
64              margin-top:0px;
65          }
66
67      </style>
```

9. The `<footer>` sits directly below the text in the `<aside>`. This needs to be styled, again by using float and setting the width to 1000 pixels, the same width as the wrapper `<div>`.

10. Next we'll apply some styling to the heading text, making them different sizes and colours. Experiment until you're happy with the results.

11. A `<footer>` tends to be separated from the main content of a page. This can be done by making it a different colour or by adding a border to the top of the `<footer>`.

Hot Tip

Keep the width of a page to a maximum of 1280 pixels to make sure that the site will look good on the vast majority of desktop screens.

GETTING ONLINE

It's no good going to all that effort to build a website and then keeping it hidden away on your computer – it needs to be out there on the web! To do this you need a domain name, a web server and an FTP Client application for managing your site's files.

DOMAIN NAME

A domain name is the human-readable name that is associated with the IP address of your website, for example, Google's domain name is google.com. This is a unique name that needs **registering** so that it is assigned to you. To do this you use a domain name **registrar** such as 1&1 (www.1and1.co.uk) or 123-reg (www.123-reg.co.uk).

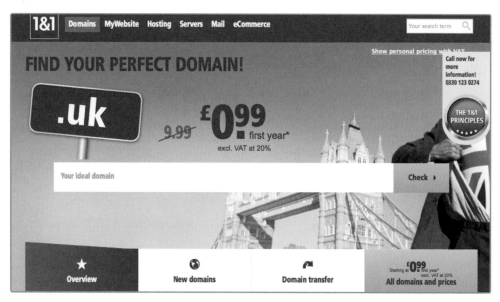

Above: 1&1 is a popular domain name registrar and hosting service provider.

WEB SERVER

Your website needs to be available on the internet, and for this you need a web server. The easiest way to get one is via a web-hosting service; this provides you with your own web server. ISPs often include such services as part of your rental package. Alternatively you can buy hosting services for a little as £1/month from the likes of 1&1 and 123-reg.

TRANSFERRING FILES

FTP (File Transfer Protocol) provides a means for transferring files across a network, and is the best method for getting your site files onto your web server. There are numerous FTP Client applications, with Filezilla (http://filezilla-project.org) and CyberDuck (http://cyberduck.io) being popular choices on Windows and Mac respectively.

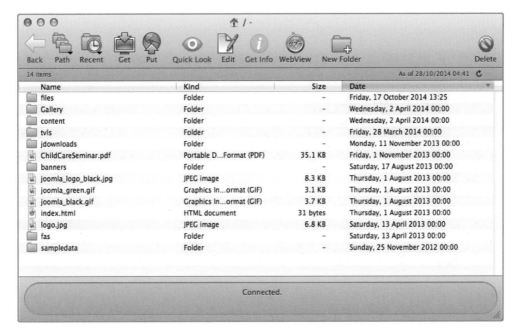

Above: An FTP Client application allows you to transfer files to and from your web server.

ADDING A BLOG TO YOUR SITE

Web logs, or blogs to give them their usual name, are a common addition to a website, and help you build a community of users with similar interests to you.

TWO EASY OPTIONS

From a programing point of view, blogs are quite complex; you've come a long way, but you're not ready to tackle that particular project just yet! Thankfully, then, you can add a blog to your site without having to build your own, and your newly acquired knowledge of HTML and CSS can be brought to bear on customizing the blog. You can either link from your site to an external blog provider, or install third-party blogging software on your web server. WordPress is a great option for both scenarios.

Below: Sign up for a free WordPress site at www.wordpress.com.

Wordpress.com

Despite having grown into a complete **CMS** (Content Management System), WordPress is, at its core, a blogging system and can still be used as such. If you wish to keep things as simple as possible then head along to www.wordpress.com and create a site with them. Follow the excellent tutorials on the site to get your blog up and running, and then link to it from your regular website.

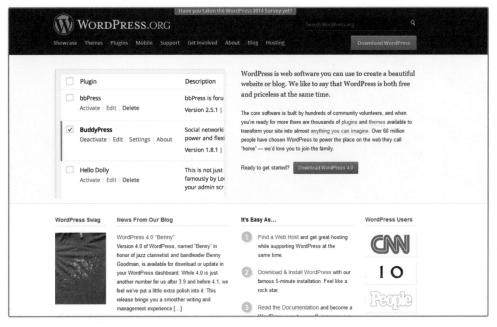

Above: The latest installable version of WordPress is at www.wordpress.org.

Wordpress.org

You can also install WordPress on your own website. Often it is provided as an option by your web server host; all you need to do is switch it on from your server control panel. Alternatively, the software can also be downloaded from www.wordpress.org if it's not offered pre-installed by your host. You can then use WordPress to create blog pages or, indeed, to run your entire site. Full documentation is available from www.wordpress.org.

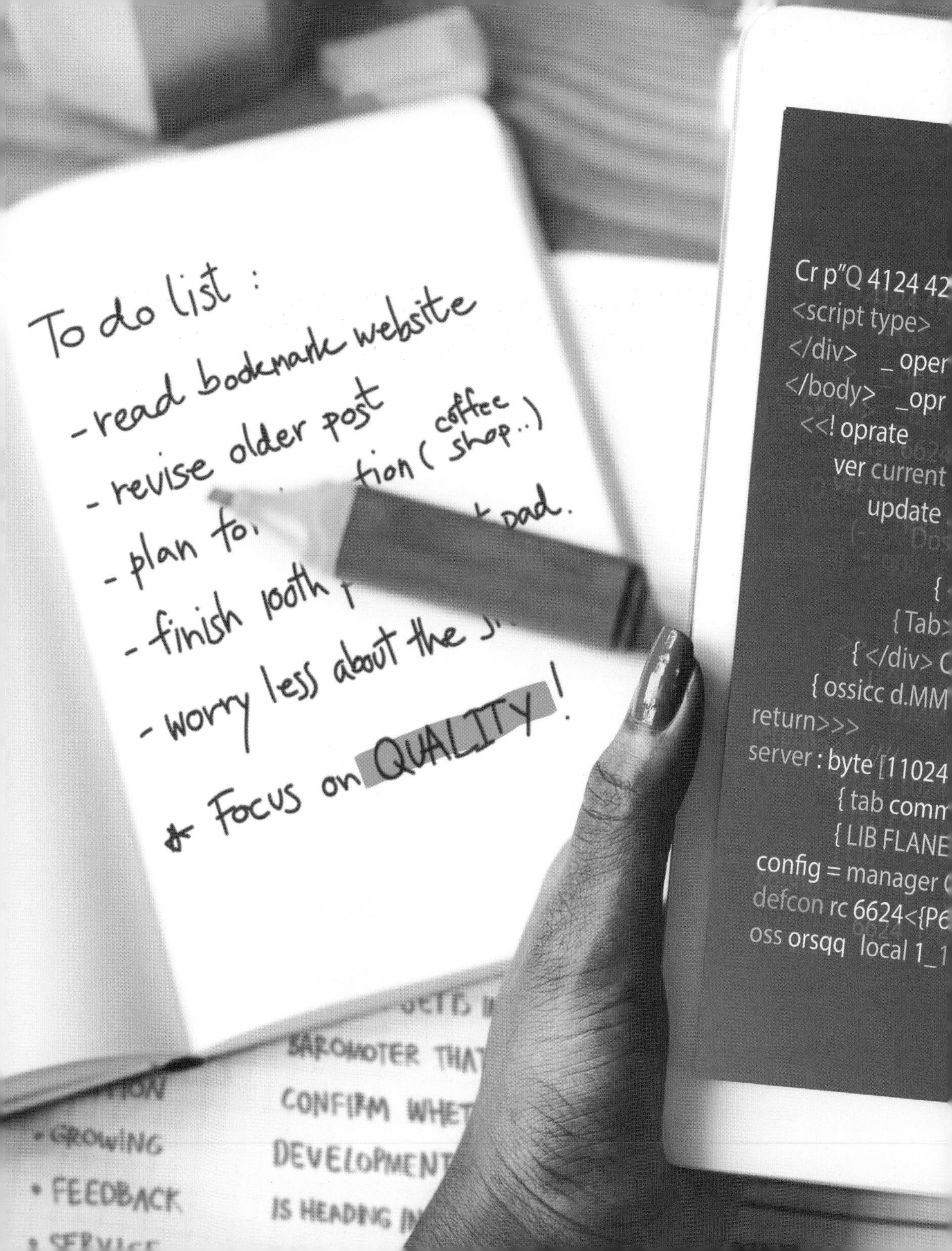

To do list :
- read bookmark website
- revise older post
- worry less about the
★ Focus on QUALITY !
<script type>
</div>
</body>
<<! oprate
ver current
update
return>>>
config = manager
oss orsqq
BAROMOTER
CONFIRM
• GROWING
DEVELOPMENT
• FEEDBACK
IS HEADING

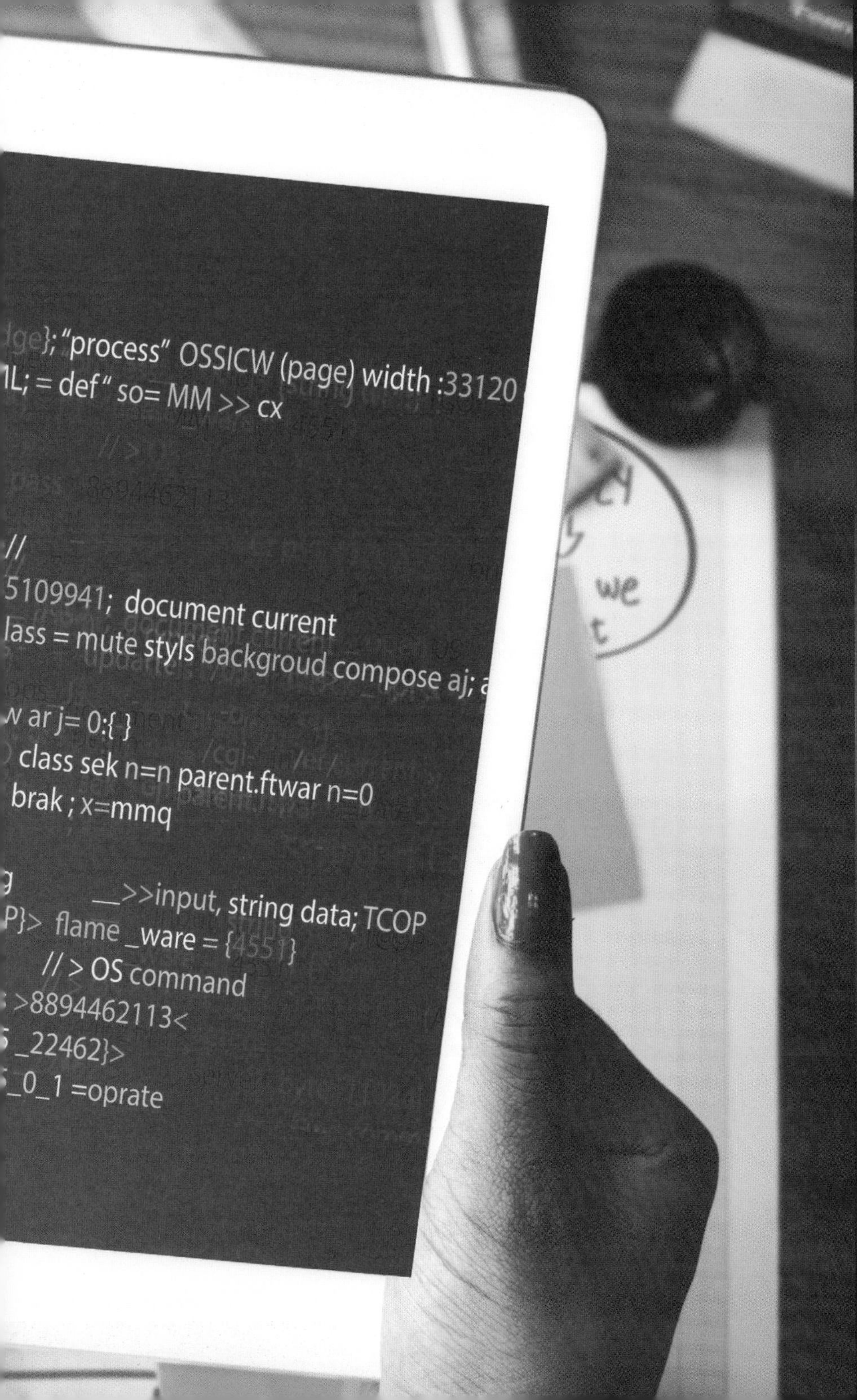

IMAGES, VIDEO & OTHER ENHANCEMENTS

ADDING MEDIA TO YOUR WEBSITE

Most websites contain a lot more than just text. Images, video and audio can greatly increase your visitor numbers and encourage them to stay longer. Advanced HTML5 features such as geolocation can improve your site's interactions with your visitors and, of course, adding a sprinkle of visual polish is always a good idea.

WORKING WITH IMAGES

Alongside text, images are the element that almost every website has in common. Very rarely will you find a contemporary website with a total lack of imagery. Images are extremely versatile and have the potential to make a website much more visually appealing.

IMAGE FORMATS

Images come in a variety of formats, but on the web there are effectively three formats used: GIF, PNG and JPG. The GIF format is a hangover from the early days of the web and is becoming increasingly uncommon. PNG and JPG, on the other hand, are widely used. Both have specific advantages and disadvantages, but together they can satisfy all situations.

The PNG Format

PNG (Portable Network Graphics, pronounced 'ping') is the best option for graphics (as opposed to photo-based imagery) because typically they use lossless compression and so offer better sharpness and accuracy than JPG. Their other benefit is that they support transparency. This means that a PNG image needn't have a solid-coloured background, and that anything behind them can show through the transparent areas of the PNG.

Below: The PNG image format is often the best for small graphic elements like logos.

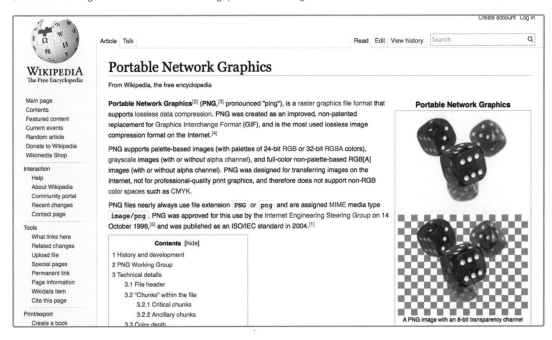

The JPG Format

The JPG format (also known as JPEG, pronounced 'jay-peg') uses a complex image compression technique to reduce the file size of an image without visibly degrading it. This means that the images can be saved at different quality levels to reduce the file size of an image. The higher the level, the better the quality, but the larger the file size; the developer can choose where to strike the balance. JPGs don't support transparency and so are not as suitable for graphics.

Hot Tip

When creating images and graphics, work from a full quality editable version in a lossless format such as PSD (Photoshop's native format), then export the graphics you need as PNG or JPG files.

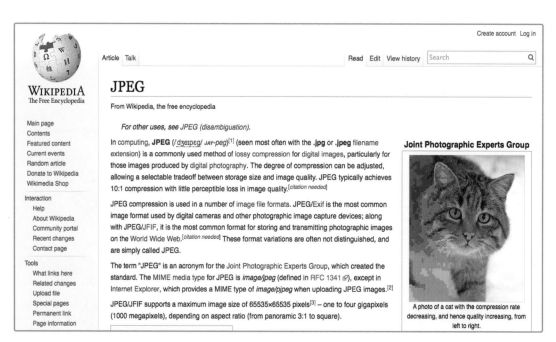

Above: Photos are usually saved in the JPG format.

ADDING IMAGES

The addition of images to a web page is a relatively simple process. However, before adding an image, it is a good idea to store your images in a sub-folder of your site root.

THE <IMG> ELEMENT

When adding images to a page we use the <img> element. This is a self-closing element, meaning that, you will recall, they only have an opening tag and no closing tag, and can't have any content nested within them.

How to Add an Image

1. In the previous chapter we built a simple page in a folder called MyFirstSite. Locate this folder and create a subfolder within it; name the subfolder 'images'.

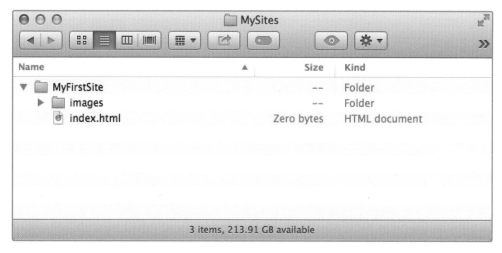

Step 1: Make sure the 'images' folder is a subfolder of the site root folder.

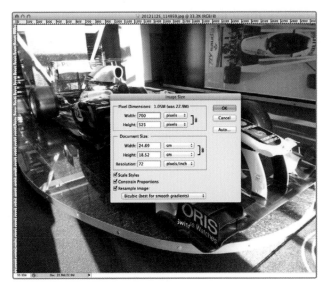

Step 2: Image editors can resize an image whilst retaining the correct proportions.

2. Find a suitable image. Use your image editor to resize it to 700 pixels wide and whatever height is proportional to that width for your chosen image. Save a copy of the image into the folder we have just created, using the JPG format. Name the file homepageImage.jpg.

3. Open your site's homepage (index. html) in your text or HTML editor, and locate the <h2> element that's at the top of the <section> element. Create an empty line in the HTML, above the <h2> element.

```
74
75      <body>
76
77          <div id="wrapper">
78              <header>
79                  <nav>Home | About | Contact </nav>
80                  <hgroup>
81                      <h1>My First Web Page</h1>
82                      <h2>It may be basic, but it rocks</h2>
83                  </hgroup>
84              </header>
85
86              <section>
87                  |
88                  <h2>Welcome To My World!</h2>
89                  <p>Lorem ipsum dolor sit amet, consectetuer adipiscing elit. Sed sagittis ante malesuada
        velit. Curabitur suscipit.</p>
90                  <p>Suspendisse quis nibh aliquam sem pulvinar sollicitudin. Etiam venenatis. Curabitur
        luctus. Nunc venenatis lacus molestie sapien. Phasellus erat. Vestibulum posuere varius dolor. Aenean id
        arcu. Sed mauris mauris, consectetuer nec, accumsan ut.</p>
91                  <p>Maecenas elementum aliquet velit!</p>
92              </section>
```

Step 3: Create an empty line in the HTML code.

```
79              <nav>Home | About | Contact </nav>
80              <hgroup>
81                  <h1>My First Web Page</h1>
82                  <h2>It may be basic, but it rocks</h2>
83              </hgroup>
84          </header>
85
86          <section>
87              <img id="homepageImage"
88                  name="Williams"
89                  alt="What a day at the Williams factory!"
90                  src="images/homepageImage.jpg"
91              />
92              <h2>Welcome To My World!</h2>
93              <p>Lorem ipsum dolor sit amet, consectetuer adipiscing elit. Sed sagittis ante malesuada
velit. Curabitur suscipit.</p>
94              <p>Suspendisse quis nibh aliquam sem pulvinar sollicitudin. Etiam venenatis. Curabitur
luctus. Nunc venenatis lacus molestie sapien. Phasellus erat. Vestibulum posuere varius dolor. Aenean id
arcu. Sed mauris mauris, consectetuer nec, accumsan ut.</p>
95              <p>Maecenas elementum aliquet velit!</p>
96          </section>
97
```

Step 4: When defining more than a couple of attributes, it's not unusual to split them into separate indented lines, making them easier to read.

4. Now add the `<img>` element as shown in the illustration. The `name` attribute value will be displayed in place of the image if the browser is unable to load it, whilst the `alt` attribute value is the text that is shown if the user hovers the mouse pointer above the image. The `src` attribute value is the URL of the image to use (note we're using a relative URL).

5. We're going to create a style rule for the image, so find the `<style>` element in the `<head>` of your page. Add the code shown in the illustration. Note that we're using an ID selector so that we target only our newly added `<img>` element. Save your work and be sure to view the results in your web browser.

```
54
55      h3 {
56          font-weight:normal;
57          font-size:18px;
58          font-style:italic;
59          color:#FF9933;
60      }
61
62      hgroup > h1 {
63          margin-bottom:3px;
64      }
65
66      hgroup > h2 {
67          margin-top:0px;
68          margin-bottom:0px;
69      }
70
71      #homepageImage {
72          float:left;
73          border-style:none;
74      }
75
76  </style>
77
```

Step 5: Some browsers draw a border around an image; use the `border-style` property to control this behaviour.

ADDING VIDEO

Video is a medium that is very commonplace in web pages and websites. They are attention-grabbing and are much more engaging than a static image. Users want to watch video, and a ten-second video clip can impart far more information than an image and text occupying the same space.

VIDEO OPTIONS

There are two main options for adding video to a web page. One is to use the `<video>` element, while the other (and simpler) option is to embed a YouTube (or similar) video into a page. In basic setups, the `<video>` element requires the actual video file to be stored on your web server. Embedding a YouTube video is simply a matter of copying and pasting code provided by YouTube.

```
1   <!DOCTYPE HTML>
2
3   <html>
4
5       <head>
6           <title>My Video Page</title>
7       </head>
8
9       <body>
10
11          <video src="videos/stoneham.mp4"></video>
12
13      </body>
14
15  </html>
16
```

Above: Adding video to a site used to be difficult; with HTML5 it's a doddle.

ADD A VIDEO WITH HTML

To embed a video into a page, add a `<video>` element to its HTML. There are two ways to specify the video file that's to be played. The simplest is to use the `<video>` element's `src` attribute, into which the video's URL is entered. However, due to the fact that different browsers support different formats of video, it's not uncommon to provide multiple versions of the video in different file formats. When doing this we have to embed a `<source>` element within the `<video>` element for each file format you provide.

Hot Tip

If hosting your own videos, favour the MP4 file format. You should also consider including a version in Ogg-Theora format to improve browser and OS compatibility (http://theora.org).

```
1   <!DOCTYPE HTML>
2
3   <html>
4
5       <head>
6           <title>My Video Page</title>
7       </head>
8
9       <body>
10
11          <video>
12              <source src="videos/stoneham.mp4" type="video/mp4">
13              <source src="videos/stoneham.ogv" type="video/ogg">
14          </video>
15
16      </body>
17
18  </html>
19
```

Above: The `<source>` element allows you to include multiple versions of a video.

Above: Embedding a YouTube video is simply a copy and paste job.

ADD A YOUTUBE VIDEO

Adding a YouTube video is much simpler than hosting your own. If it's a video you've produced yourself then you will need a Google account to allow you to upload the material to YouTube. Once there, though, hooking your video into your page couldn't be easier.

The <iframe> Element

All videos on YouTube have a button underneath them marked Share. Clicking this button reveals a panel with three tabs along the top and a field containing some code. Clicking the Embed tab will generate the HTML code for an <iframe>, an element that creates a portal between your site and another. Copy the <iframe> code and paste it into your page's HTML: simple!

ADDING AUDIO

HTML5's new `<audio>` element works on very much the same principle as `<video>`. As with `<video>`, the `<audio>` element supports multiple source files in order to improve browser and OS compatibility.

AUDIO FORMATS

Whilst you may think MP3 audio files are ubiquitous, licensing considerations mean they are not supported in all browsers on all operating systems (it is the same situation with video, as already alluded to). Including your audio content in both MP3 and Ogg-Vorbis formats should cover all the bases, though.

Hot Tip

The Ogg-Vorbis audio format is partner to the Ogg-Theora video format. Both are open-source software and are therefore free to use. Pop along to http://vorbis.com for information and encoding tools.

```
4
5      <head>
6          <title>My Video Page</title>
7      </head>
8
9      <body>
10
11         <audio src="music/TheSentinel.mp3"></audio>
12
13         <audio>
14             <source src="music/TheSentinel.mp3" type="audio/mp3">
15             <source src="music/TheSentinel.oga" type="audio/ogg">
16         </audio>
17
18     </body>
19
```

Above: Including audio content in a page is a doddle with the `<audio>` element.

GOING BEYOND THE BASICS

HTML5 and CSS3 represent significant advances in their respective languages. Here we introduce some of the more advanced features of both languages. A full discussion is beyond the scope of this book, but you should be aware of these features.

HTML5 FORMS

A simple example of the power of HTML5 lies in HTML forms. Before HTML5, creating forms for the web typically involved the use of coding with **JavaScrip**t. For instance, if you wished to verify that the user had entered suitable data into a **form** the only way to do so was via scripting. HTML5 forms, however, have built-in validation features, saving the developer heaps of time and complexity.

Below: HTML5 forms greatly simplify validation of user entries.

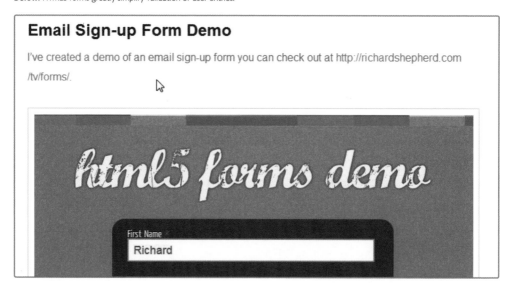

Email Sign-up Form Demo

I've created a demo of an email sign-up form you can check out at http://richardshepherd.com /tv/forms/.

html5 forms demo

First Name

Richard

HTML5 DRAG-AND-DROP

Drag-and-drop is fundamental to computer use, and is a very intuitive way for a user to interact with on-screen objects. In HTML5, adding the `draggable` attribute to any visual element and setting the attribute's value to `"true"` makes that element draggable: `<img id="#homepageImage" draggable="true" />`. Handling such interactions remains the job of a scripting language like JavaScript.

Above: The user will be asked whether or not they wish to share their geolocation data with your site.

HTML5 GEOLOCATION

The HTML5 geolocation feature is used to determine a person's location through their desktop or mobile device. A popular use of geolocation is on mobile devices where it integrates with maps. It is used for a host of services that need your location, for example, for getting directions from A to B.

CSS TRANSFORMS

Transforms manipulate the visual appearance of HTML elements. For example, the `rotate` style property will rotate an element. This makes it easy to turn a square into a diamond, for example. Other properties include `scale` and `skew`. The former makes an element larger, whilst the latter tilts an element.

CSS TRANSITIONS

Transitions allow elements to change visually over a specified time period. A simple example of the transition property is typically found on buttons. These will have an initial background colour which fades to another colour when the mouse cursor is hovered over the button. Used subtly, such effects add a touch of class to a site.

```
7
8        <style>
9            div {
10               position:absolute;
11               width:100px;
12               height:100px;
13               background-color:red;
14           }
15
16           #box {
17               left:200px;
18               top:200px;
19           }
20
21           #rotatedBox {
22               left:400px;
23               top:200px;
24               transform:rotate(45deg);
25           }
26       </style>
27
```

Left & Above: Transforms allow the position and orientation of elements to be adjusted.

How Transitions Work

We already know how to use Pseudo-Class selectors to make an < a > element respond to different states, such as : hover, when the mouse pointer is over an element. What you may not realize is that Pseudo-Class selectors can operate on any visual element. This is the key to triggering a transition; we define it within a Pseudo-Class selector's style rule.

For example, if we had an element with an id of "homeButton", then we could target a specific style rule at this button when the mouse is over it using an ID selector. We would then define the transition within the style rule (see illustration).

```
19
20
21          #homeButton:hover {
22              transition-property:background-colour;
23              transition-duration:0.6s;
24              transition-timing-function:ease;
25              background-color:blue;
26          }
27
28
```

Above: There are a number of style properties that, taken together, define the transition.

CSS KEYFRAMES

Keyframes are a concept from the world of animation. They specify a point in time and the state of an object at that point – the intermediate steps between the keyframes can then be calculated by the computer. Until HTML5 and CSS3 came along, Adobe Flash was the standard for creating keyframed animations on a web page, but not any more!

Apply an Animation

Animations can be applied to almost every element in a web page. Here we are going to demonstrate how to animate a `<div>` element moving across the screen.

Hot Tip

Related groups of CSS properties often have a shorthand equivalent that can set all such properties in one line of code. For example, the various animation-style properties can be declared simultaneously via the `animation` **property.**

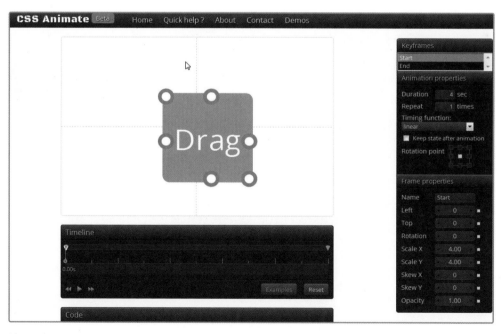

Above: CSS animation changes the value of a style property over time.

Creating a Simple Animation

1. Create a new HTML document, add the basic structural elements (<html>, <head> and <body>) and create a <style> element in the <head>. Save the file as movingbox.html.

2. Add a <div> within the body and give it an id of 'boxToMove'. In the <style> element create an ID selector and define a style rule that will size the <div> to 100 x 100 pixels and give it a background colour so we can see it on-screen.

3. We'll now add the animation code to the style rule. Copy the style properties and values from the illustration; the style property names are self-explanatory.

Hot Tip

Not all browsers support keyframe animation – if it's not working for you, try opening the page in Firefox.

```
1   <!DOCTYPE HTML>
2
3   <html>
4
5       <head>
6           <title>CSS Animation</title>
7           <style>
8           </style>
9       </head>
10
11      <body>
12
13      </body>
14
15  </html>
16
```

Step 1: Create a basic document called movingbox.html.

```
7       <style>
8
9           #boxToMove {
10              position:relative;
11              width:100px;
12              height:100px;
13              background-color:red;
14              animation-name:boxMover;
15              animation-duration:3s;
16              animation-iteration-count:infinite;
17          }
18
19
20      </style>
```

Steps 2 & 3: The style rules define both the appearance of the movingbox <div>, and its animation properties.

4.   The final part of the jigsaw is the keyframe code. This is declared in a way we have not yet investigated, using a CSS '@' declaration, in this case @keyframes. This is followed by the name of the animation, the same name as is declared in the animation-name style property.

```
7          <style>
8
9              #boxToMove {
10                 position:relative;
11                 width:100px;
12                 height:100px;
13                 background-color:red;
14                 animation-name:boxMover;
15                 animation-duration:3s;
16                 animation-iteration-count:infinite;
17             }
18
19             @keyframes boxMover {
20                 0%    {top:0px;}
21                 25%   {top:100px;}
22                 75%   {top:50px;}
23                 100% {top:150px;}
24             }
```

Steps 4 & 5: The code following the @keyframes declaration defines which style properties will be animated, and what values they'll take at various points in time.

5.   The lines of code that follow the @keyframes declaration define a style property and value against various points in time, expressed as percentages. The top style property we are using determines the distance between the top of the animated element and the top of its containing block, in this case the <body> element.

6.   Save your work and open the file in a browser to see the results.

HTML AND JAVASCRIPT

We already know that HTML creates the structure for a page and defines its content, and that CSS controls the visual look of that content. Scripting completes this picture by providing the means to control the behaviour of your page, and how it reacts to user interaction. There are various scripting languages for the web, but the main one – built into all web browsers – is JavaScript.

WHERE DOES JAVASCRIPT FIT?

Earlier we used the analogy of a house to describe HTML and CSS, the former being the bricks and mortar, and the latter being the decoration and finish. If we stick with this analogy, JavaScript (or JS for short) would be a smart-house control system that can control every aspect of the house intricately.

Right: JavaScript is the most common scripting language used in web pages.

Adding a Script

The intricacies of JavaScript are explored in the later chapters of this book, but let's take a quick look at how you add a script to a page, to get us started. For a more detailed look at this see page 142.

The <script> Element

Like CSS, a script can be embedded into your page or be external to your page. The latter is the more common approach, but both are achieved via the <script> element: an embedded script is written between the opening and closing <script> tags; an external script is located in a separate text file and is linked to a page using the src attribute of the <script> element.

Below: Like CSS, scripts can be embedded or external.

```
 5    <head>
 6        <title>Script Elements</title>
 7
 8        <!--This is an external script...-->
 9        <script type="text/javascript" src="js/siteCore.js"></script>
10
11        <!--This is an embedded script...-->
12        <script type="text/javascript">
13            var com;
14            if(!com) {
15                com = {};
16            }
17            if(!com.ukmastersdvd) {
18                com.ukmastersdvd = {};
19            }
20
21            com.ukmastersdvd.resetContactForm = function() {
22                document.getElementById("messageTitle").setAttribute("value", "");
23                document.getElementById("messageTitleMessage").textContent = "";
24                document.getElementById("senderAddress").setAttribute("value", "");
25                document.getElementById("senderAddressMessage").textContent = "";
26                document.getElementById("messageBody").textContent = "";
27                document.getElementById("messageBodyMessage").textContent = "";
28            }
29
30        </script>
31
32    </head>
```

Execute on Sight

A `<script>` element can appear anywhere within a web page, and is executed – in other words, run – when the browser encounters it (*see page 143*). Typically, then, scripts that have to be available to the whole page are defined in the `<head>`, whereas scripts that create an output to the page whilst the page is being rendered are positioned at the location that the output is required.

A GOOD UNDERSTANDING

A thorough understanding of JavaScript allows you to take your site well beyond the limitations of HTML and CSS, turning your pages into bona fide web applications, but it's a deep subject with a lot to learn. In later chapters of this book (*see page 134*) we explore JavaScript, providing you with an excellent place to start learning about this fascinating and complex language.

ADVANCED HTML & CSS CODING

ADVANCED TEXT

As we have learned, HTML is nothing more than plain text; it only works at all because web browsers recognize characters that have a special meaning in HTML, such as '<' and '>'. But what if we want to use one of those special characters within the text of a page?

SPECIAL CHARACTERS

There are a number of characters that, if typed into a text-based element such as <p>, will cause errors and the page will not be rendered correctly (if at all). For example, we may wish to include angle brackets in a passage about mathematical formulae (or, indeed, HTML), or quote marks when quoting what somebody has said. The problem is that such characters have specific predefined meanings in HTML and so will be misinterpreted by the browser.

Special Characters

"There are many special characters in HTML" said the man. "Characters such as '<' & '>' can't be typed directly into the text of an HTML document." he said.

He went on to explain that the same was true of "extended" characters such as ©, μ and many more. Accented latin characters, such as 'Á' and 'È' are also classed as extended characters, he explained.

Above: Some characters have special meaning in HTML and can't be typed directly into an element.

ASCII and Extended Characters

The core set of character symbols used in computing is referred to as **ASCII** (American Standard Code for Information Interchange, pronounced 'ask-ee'). This is a standard that defines the **character code** used to represent the most common alphabetic, numeric and punctuation characters. There are 128 such character codes, and all computers follow the ASCII standard for these character codes. Characters that fall outside of the ASCII standard, such as accented letters, are known as **extended** characters and shouldn't be typed directly into HTML text.

Right: All computers use the ASCII standard to represent basic letters, numbers and punctuation.

> # Hot Tip
>
> **Internally, computers represent everything with numbers, and this includes text. The number that represents a given alpha-numeric, punctuation or symbol character is called a character code.**

ASCII control characters

00	NULL	(Null character)
01	SOH	(Start of Header)
02	STX	(Start of Text)
03	ETX	(End of Text)
04	EOT	(End of Trans.)
05	ENQ	(Enquiry)
06	ACK	(Acknowledgement)
07	BEL	(Bell)
08	BS	(Backspace)
09	HT	(Horizontal Tab)
10	LF	(Line feed)
11	VT	(Vertical Tab)
12	FF	(Form feed)
13	CR	(Carriage return)
14	SO	(Shift Out)
15	SI	(Shift In)
16	DLE	(Data link escape)
17	DC1	(Device control 1)
18	DC2	(Device control 2)
19	DC3	(Device control 3)
20	DC4	(Device control 4)
21	NAK	(Negative acknowl.)
22	SYN	(Synchronous idle)
23	ETB	(End of trans. block)
24	CAN	(Cancel)
25	EM	(End of medium)
26	SUB	(Substitute)
27	ESC	(Escape)
28	FS	(File separator)
29	GS	(Group separator)
30	RS	(Record separator)
31	US	(Unit separator)
127	DEL	(Delete)

ASCII printable characters

32	space	64	@	96	`
33	!	65	A	97	a
34	"	66	B	98	b
35	#	67	C	99	c
36	$	68	D	100	d
37	%	69	E	101	e
38	&	70	F	102	f
39	'	71	G	103	g
40	(	72	H	104	h
41	)	73	I	105	i
42	*	74	J	106	j
43	+	75	K	107	k
44	,	76	L	108	l
45	-	77	M	109	m
46	.	78	N	110	n
47	/	79	O	111	o
48	0	80	P	112	p
49	1	81	Q	113	q
50	2	82	R	114	r
51	3	83	S	115	s
52	4	84	T	116	t
53	5	85	U	117	u
54	6	86	V	118	v
55	7	87	W	119	w
56	8	88	X	120	x
57	9	89	Y	121	y
58	:	90	Z	122	z
59	;	91	[	123	{
60	<	92	\	124		
61	=	93	]	125	}
62	>	94	^	126	~
63	?	95	_		

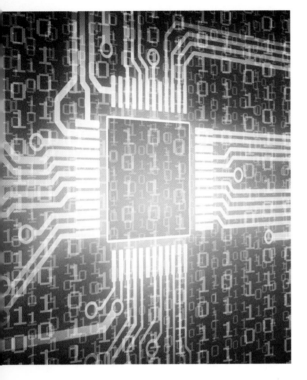

CHARACTER ENTITIES

The solution to both of these scenarios is something called **character entities**. To use these you type a special little bit of code into the HTML text which, when rendered, will be displayed as the desired character. All special characters and many extended characters have their own dedicated character entity.

How to Write a Character Entity

Character entities consist of an ampersand '&' followed by an entity name, such as 'quot', and are rounded off with a semicolon ';'. So, to create a quote character, we type " rather than typing an actual quote mark. Interestingly, because an ampersand is itself a special character, you have to write & to make one appear in the rendered text of your page.

```
26      <body>
27          <header>
28              <h1>Special Characters</h1>
29          </header>
30          <section>
31              <p>&quot;There are many special characters in HTML&quot; said the man. &quot;
Characters such as '&lt;' &amp; '&gt;' can't be typed directly into the text of an HTML
document.&quot; he said.</p>
32              <p>He went on to explain that the same was true of &quot;extended&quot;
characters such as &copy;, , &micro; and many more. Accented latin characters, such as '
&Aacute;' and '&Egrave;' are also classed as extended characters, he explained.</p>
33          </section>
34
35      </body>
```

Above: All special and many extended characters are represented by character entities.

Unnamed Entities

Not all extended characters have a predefined character entity, so how do we include such a character in a page? This time we have to use a character code reference instead of an entity name – it looks like this: © (this would be a '©' character). The '#' states that what follows is a character code and the 'x' states that the code is being supplied in **Unicode** format. A discussion of Unicode is beyond the scope of this book, but you can look up the code for any character at http://unicode-table.com/en/.

Hot Tip

There are many different character entity names. If your HTML editor supports code hinting then this will help you find the one you want. Otherwise, keep a bookmark somewhere handy that points to http://dev.w3.org/html5/html-author/charref.

```
26      <body>
27          <header>
28              <h1>Special Characters</h1>
29          </header>
30          <section>
31              <p>&quot;There are many special characters in HTML&quot; said the man. &quot;
        Characters such as '&lt;' &amp; '&' can't be typed directly into the text of an HTML
        document.&quot; he said.</p>
32              <p>He went on to expla        e was true of &quot;extended&quot;
        characters such as &copy;, &micro;        Accented latin characters, such as '
        &Aacute;' and '&Egrave;' are also        ded characters, he explained.</p>
33          </section>
34
35      </body>
```

Above: Code hinting can be a huge help in finding the desired character entity.

ADAPTIVE LAYOUTS

Building websites is no longer a case of creating a website that looks good on a desktop computer. Mobile devices – smartphones and tablets – are now widely used for web browsing, and this has an impact on how we lay out and style web pages.

```
10      body {
11          font-family:"Lato";
12          font-size:14px;
13      }
14
15      #wrapper {
16          width:80%;
17          height:auto;
18          margin-left:auto;
19          margin-right:auto;
20      }
21
22      section {
23          width:70%;
24          height:auto;
25          float:left;
26      }
27
28      aside {
29          width:30%;
30          float:left;
31      }
32
33      footer {
34          width:100%;
35          height:auto;
36          float:left;
37          background-color:lightgray;
38          border-top:1px solid gray;
39          padding-left:1%;
40          padding-bottom:1%;
41      }
```

FIT TO ALL SCREENS

There are several options when it comes to making a site for all screens, big and small. One approach that has been around since the early days of the internet is proportional – *aka* 'liquid' – layouts. When using this technique we express positions and dimensions in percentage terms. This causes the layout to scale to the size of the browser window.

Left: Expressing dimensions and positions as percentages is one way to make your pages adapt to the browser window's dimensions.

CREATING A LIQUID LAYOUT

When creating a `<div>` or other structural element, it
is common to specify a width for it in absolute terms, for
example, `1000px` ('px' is the code you use in CSS to
denote pixels). If the browser window's width is less than
this then some of the page will spill over the edges and
won't be visible without scrolling.

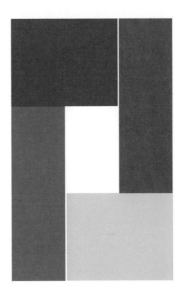

Stating sizes in percentages solves this problem to a certain
degree because it keeps things in proportion: if a `<div>`
element's width is set to 80% then it will always be 80 per cent
of the width of its containing block. Throw together a few
coloured `<div>` elements in a page to see how this works.

Above & below: This arrangement of `<div>` elements highlights how liquid layouts work.

```
2
3   <html>
4
5       <head>
6           <title>Untitled Document</title>
7       </head>
8
9       <body>
10
11          <header>
12              <!--The header element's containing block is the body element-->
13
14              <p>This p element's containing block is the header element</p>
15
16              <p>This is an inline image: <img src="images/myImage.jpg"/>
17                  it's a child of the p element</p>
18              <!--The containing block of the img element is also the
19              header because a p doesn't form a block-->
20
21          </header>
22
23      </body>
24
25  </html>
26
```

Above: Every visual element has a containing block that is used as the reference point for sizing and positioning.

Hot Tip

An element's containing block is the nearest ancestor of that element that can be used as a reference point for sizing and positioning.

Problems with Liquid Layouts

The liquid layout technique was developed at a time before mobile devices and was intended to cope with the lower resolution monitors that computers tended to have back then. It is becoming something of a relic, though, because modern monitors are normally perfectly big enough to accommodate the largest of designs. Liquid layouts do not work especially well on mobile devices either; this being due to the way such devices internally manage screen scaling. The modern approach, then, is to craft your page so that it will display well on *any* device whether mobile or desktop.

RESPONSIVE WEB DESIGN

Responsive Web Design, also known as RWD, is a technique for making a page or site adapt automatically to the type and size of device on which it is being viewed.

MEDIA QUERIES

Responsive Web Design is powered by what are known as **media queries**. These are a component of CSS that allow you to use values that aren't determined until the page is loaded into a browser. So instead of setting a `<header>` element to be, say, 1000 pixels wide, you could set it to always match the width of the browser window, no matter how wide that window, like this:

```
header {width:device-width;}
```

Below: The Boston Globe's website is one of the original examples of Responsive Web Design.

DIFFERENT DEVICES, DIFFERENT STYLE SHEETS

Desktop, tablet and smartphone screens are all of different widths and resolutions. The way to deal with this is to create multiple versions of a style sheet, each one tailored to support a specific class of device. The browser will then select a sheet based on the `<style>`/`<link>` element's `media` attribute value.

```
 8
 9      <link
10          rel="stylesheet"
11          type="text/css"
12          href="handheldSmall.css"
13          media="handheld and max-device-width:480px"
14      />
15
16      <link
17          rel="stylesheet"
18          type="text/css"
19          href="handheldLarge.css"
20          media="handheld and min-device-width:481px"
21      />
22
23      <style media="all and not handheld">
24
25
26          body {
27              font-family:"Lato";
28              font-size:14px;
29          }
30
31          #wrapper {
32              width:1000px;
33              height:auto;
```

Above: The browser can select a style sheet based on the type of device it is running on.

Same Meat, Different Gravy

The various style sheets will all contain the same selectors, and the same style properties will be used in each selector's style rule. What will be different are the values assigned to the style properties. This means that the entire layout of your page will adapt itself to the user's device.

GETTING HELP
TO GO RESPONSIVE

There are a number of frameworks available that will take much of the hard work out of the process of building your own RWD site, so if you want to try your hand at it then check out the following tools.

FRAMEWORKS

The two most popular and best-featured RWD frameworks are Foundation and Bootstrap. They provide all of the necessary resources required to build an RWD site: menus, image sliders, buttons and much more. Take a look at both to see which you prefer.

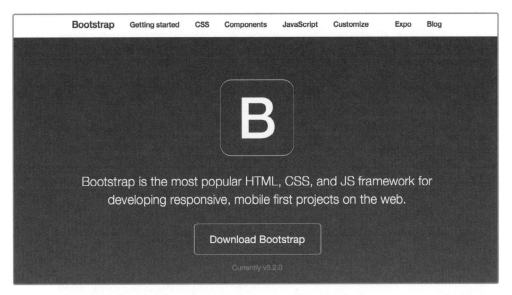

Above: Get started with Bootstrap by downloading and experimenting with it (http://getbootstrap.com).

Responsive Templates

Frameworks are the perfect solution for those who want to create a responsive website, but you still need to learn how to use them. A simpler and quicker solution is to use ready-made templates, leaving you with little more to do than add text and images to create a complete site. Try HTML5 UP (http://html5up.net) for some modern templates.

RWD Tool to Try

When creating a website, it's essential to test it on as many screens as possible, but with the plethora of different screen sizes out there this is not always feasible. There are many tools that can help by simulating different device screens on your desktop. Screenfly is a great example of such a tool; check it out at http://quirktools.com/screenfly.

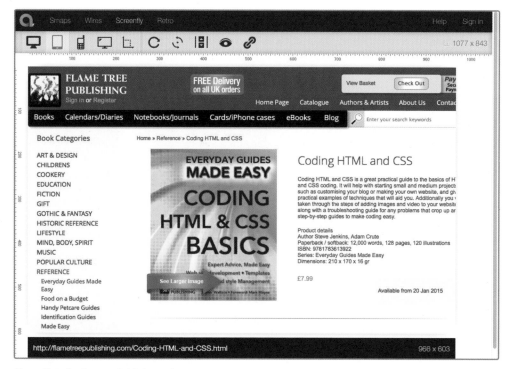

Above: Test a live site on myriad devices and screens.

CONTROLLING MOBILE BROWSER SCALING

Web browsers running on mobile devices behave quite differently to a desktop browser when it comes to sizing a page. This is due to the way in which mobile devices scale between their physical resolution and an internal viewport size.

THE VIEWPORT

A mobile browser's viewport is the area in which it renders the visual content of the page. When the page loads, this viewport is scaled with the aim of making the viewport fit within the physical dimensions of the device's screen. When you zoom in and out with a nip of your fingers, you're actually adjusting the viewport scaling, and when you scroll around the page you're actually moving the viewport around.

Right: The viewport can, and often does, extend beyond the visible area of the screen.

The Viewport Meta Tag

In order to have the browser adopt a suitable initial scaling for the viewport, we have to let it know what size we want it to assume; if we don't do this then a default value will be used which may or may not be suitable. We set the scaling via a `<meta>` tag placed in the `<head>` of the page.

Viewport Properties

The thing we are interested in is the value of the `content` attribute. This is used to set a viewport property; in our example we are telling the viewport to match the physical width of the device. Available properties are: `width`, `height`, `minimum-scale`, `maximum-scale`, `initial-scale` and `user-scalable`.

```
5    <head>
6
7        <meta name="viewport" content="width=device-width">
8
9        <title>My First Web Page</title>
```

Above: The viewport meta tag defines the initial scaling employed by a mobile browser.

BROWSER SUPPORT

There is a host of browsers for desktop and mobile, all offering different levels of support for HTML5 and CSS3. On the desktop the major browsers are Chrome, Firefox, Internet Explorer and Safari, so you should aim to test all of your sites in at least these four browsers.

WHICH BROWSERS SHOULD I SUPPORT?

There is no doubt that Chrome, Firefox, Internet Explorer, Safari and even Opera should be supported on the desktop. The question is which version should you support? As a general rule, encourage visitors to your site to install and use the latest version of their preferred browser(s).

Hot Tip

Download and install the main browsers so that you can test your pages in each one.

Browser Compatibility Test		Web Design Gallery		Icon Search Engine		
Enter URL Here: www.bbc.co.uk					**Submit**	

Linux		Windows			Mac	BSD
☐ Arora 0.1	☑ Iceape 2.7	☑ Chrome 10.0	☑ Chrome 35.0	☑ Firefox 17.0	☑ Camino 2.1	**Contribute**
☑ Arora 0.11	☑ Iceweasel 3.5	☑ Chrome 12.0	☑ Chrome 36.0	☑ Firefox 18.0	☑ Chrome 34.0	
☑ Chrome 27.0	☑ Kazehakase 0.5	☑ Chrome 13.0	☑ Firefox 1.5	☑ Firefox 19.0	☑ Chrome 35.0	**Free 7-Day Trial**
☑ Chrome 30.0	☑ Konqueror 4.11	☑ Chrome 14.0	☑ Firefox 2.0	☑ Firefox 20.0	☑ Firefox 25.0	Largest set of VM machines anywhere
☑ Chrome 31.0	☑ Konqueror 4.4	☑ Chrome 17.0	☐ Firefox 3.0	☑ Firefox 21.0	☑ Firefox 26.0	Test your site in as few as two clicks
☑ Chrome 35.0	☑ Konqueror 4.8	☑ Chrome 18.0	☑ Firefox 3.5	☑ Firefox 22.0	☑ Firefox 27.0	**CrossBrowserTesting**
☑ Chrome 37.0	☑ Konqueror 4.9	☑ Chrome 19.0	☑ Firefox 4.0	☑ Firefox 23.0	☑ Firefox 28.0	
☑ Dillo 3.0	☑ Links 2.7	☑ Chrome 20.0	☑ Firefox 5.0	☑ Firefox 24.0	☑ Firefox 29.0	
☑ Epiphany 3.10	☐ Luakit 1.1	☑ Chrome 21.0	☑ Firefox 6.0	☑ Firefox 25.0	☑ Firefox 30.0	
☑ Epiphany 3.4	☐ Luakit 1.6	☑ Chrome 22.0	☑ Firefox 7.0	☑ Firefox 26.0	☑ Firefox 31.0	
☑ Epiphany 3.6	☑ Luakit 1.8	☑ Chrome 23.0	☑ Firefox 8.0	☑ Firefox 27.0	☑ Firefox 32.0	
☐ Firefox 3.0	☑ Lynx 2.8	☑ Chrome 24.0	☑ Firefox 9.0	☑ Firefox 28.0	☑ Opera 21.0	

Above: A browser compatibility tool like Browsershots can help you test your site.

TROUBLESHOOTING COMMON HTML/CSS PROBLEMS

When working with web-based technologies, there will always be issues of compatibility. Here we run through some of the common issues that you are likely to encounter when building websites.

WEB PAGE DOESN'T DISPLAY PROPERLY IN INTERNET EXPLORER

Older versions of Internet Explorer use a different method to other browsers to display certain HTML and CSS elements. However, the latest versions of Internet Explorer are much more standards-compliant than previous ones. The best workaround is to keep code as simple as possible.

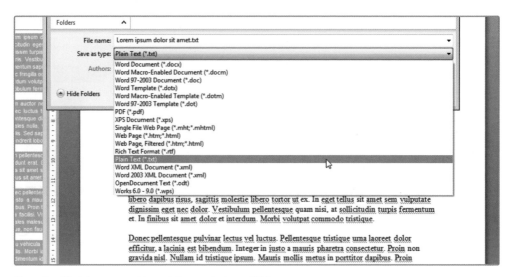

Above: Save Word documents as plain text before copying into an HTML page.

COPYING TEXT FROM WORD LEAVES LOADS OF EXTRA TEXT

Copying text directly from a Word document into a web page will also bring in a load of the styling that Word applies to its documents. You could delete this by hand, but this is time-consuming. A simple solution is to save the Word document as a text-only file and then copy and paste the text into a web page.

WHY ISN'T MY IMAGE SHOWING?

There could be a number of reasons but the first port of call is to make sure that the image's URL is using the correct path, name and file extension. You might be using a URL with the right image name but the wrong file extension, for example, png instead of jpg, or not have provided the correct folder path information.

HOW DO I CHECK THAT MY HTML IS CORRECT?

The best way to check your HTML and CSS for errors is to use an online validation tool such as the official W3C validator at http://validator.w3.org/. If you use an HTML editor such as Dreamweaver to build your pages, it will have validation tools built in.

W3C Markup Validation Service
Check the markup (HTML, XHTML,...) of Web documents

Validate by URI   Validate by File Upload   Validate by Direct Input

Validate by URI

Validate a document online:

Address: _____

▸ More Options

[Check]

This validator checks the markup validity of Web documents in HTML, XHTML, SMIL, MathML, etc. If you wish to validate specific content such as RSS/Atom feeds or CSS stylesheets, MobileOK content, or to find broken links, there are other validators and tools available. As an alternative you can also try our non-DTD-based validator.

W3C VALIDATOR Suite Try now the W3C Validator Suite™ premium service that checks your entire website and evaluates its conformance with W3C open standards to quickly identify those portions of your website that need your attention.

I ♥ VALIDATOR   The W3C validators rely on community support for hosting and development. Donate and help us build better tools for a better web.

5004

Above: Use a validation tool or service to test your HTML.

WHY ISN'T MY CODE WORKING ON MY DESKTOP?

You might have all your HTML and CSS in place and working well, but when you add some new code and test on your desktop find that nothing happens. The first step is to check that any code or scripts are pointing to the right location. If all is fine in that department, upload the page to your web server and test it from there – some code only works when it is running from a server.

IMAGES ARE LOADING VERY SLOWLY

It is not uncommon for users to place images with large file sizes onto a web page and then resize them with CSS. Multiply this by ten images and everything slows to a crawl.

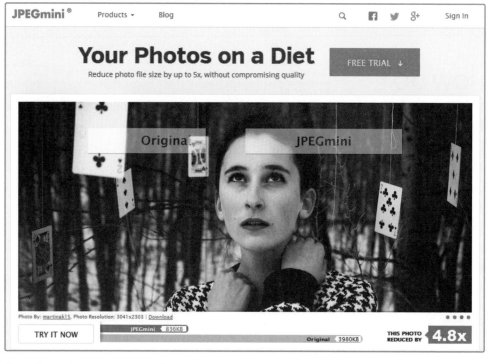

Above: Use an online image optimizer to reduce image sizes.

Try optimizing any images you are using; if you don't have an image editor then the JPEGmini online service will do the trick – *http://www.jpegmini.com*.

SOME OF MY LINKS AREN'T WORKING

Links are critical to site navigation, and so broken links can be a big problem. The first thing to check is that the <a> element and its href attribute's URL are both written correctly – if there is one mistake in the URL it won't work. If you are using a relative URL then changing to an absolute one (starting with http://) can solve the problem.

FONT ISSUES

Computers come with fonts such as Arial, Helvetica and Georgia installed. However, if you are using a different font it may not be available on the user's computer and so a substitute will be used. Web fonts get around this, but the correct code must be added in the right place. Use Google Fonts – *https://www.google.com/fonts* – for peace of mind.

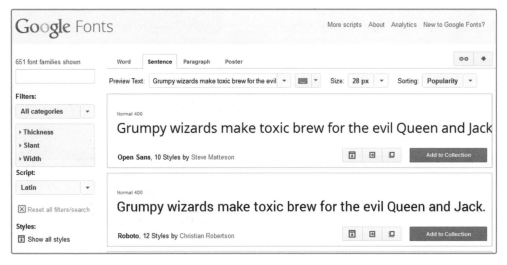

Above: Google Fonts offers hundreds of different fonts.

MEET JAVASCRIPT

JAVASCRIPT, HTML AND CSS

There are three core languages used to develop web pages: HTML provides the underlying structure and content; CSS provides the visual scenery; while JavaScript ...? Well, JavaScript provides the magic that brings the whole thing to life.

BEFORE WE START

This chapter and the proceeding chapters are concerned solely with JavaScript, yet the language is so deeply tied to web browsers and web pages that it is impossible to discuss it without relying heavily on prior knowledge of HTML and CSS. If you don't already have such knowledge, or if you're a bit rusty on the subjects, it is in your best interest to read the chapters in this book on HTML and CSS.

Right: If you didn't start at the beginning, previous chapters of this book will help you to understand JavaScript.

Hot Tip

If, in the context of HTML and CSS, you understand the meaning of terms such as element, attribute, opening and closing tags, selectors and style rules, you're good to go with JavaScript.

BROWSER COMPATIBILITY

While the core JavaScript language is fully supported across all major browsers, problems can arise when using advanced or esoteric functions, because not all browsers support all of JavaScript's extended functionality. There are ways and means to work around such issues but, unfortunately, there isn't room to cover them here.

Hot Tip

See page 13 to find out how to download completed versions of all the book's code examples. They include additional notes that help to further explain the examples.

Firefox

All of the examples in this book use standard JavaScript programming techniques and constructs. However, in order to sidestep any irksome browser compatibility issues, we'll be using the Firefox browser for running all examples, and encourage you to do the same.

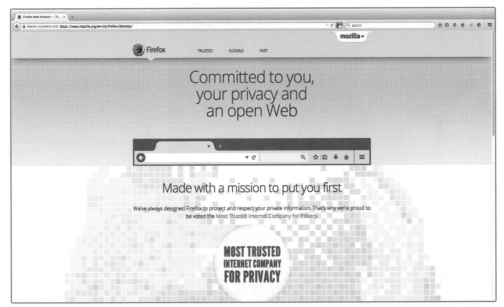

Above: Mozilla Firefox is one of the most standards-compliant web browsers currently available, and is free to install and use. You can download it from www.mozilla.org.

WHAT IS JAVASCRIPT?

JavaScript is a scripting language used to interact with and control pages loaded into a web browser. It provides a rich palette of functionality for interacting with the user, the page and the internet.

WHAT IS A SCRIPT?

In the theatre world, a script can be thought of as a series of instructions that tell the actors the actors where to be, what to do and say, and when to do and say it. In computing, the meaning is very similar: a script is a series of instructions for the computer to perform. Yes, the actors are onscreen graphics and chunks of data rather than a troupe of thespians, but the principle remains the same.

Left: A script tells the actors where to be, what to do and when to do it – the actors being computer data and graphics, of course.

JAVASCRIPT RUNS ON THE CLIENT SIDE

It's important to understand from the get-go that when using JavaScript in a web page, it runs on the user's – or client's – computer and interacts with a copy of the web page that is loaded into a web browser on that computer. This is often referred to as 'client-side' scripting.

Java and JavaScript

You may have heard of a language called Java, and think that it somehow relates to JavaScript – it doesn't. Java was a hot topic at the time JavaScript was developed, and by calling the language JavaScript, its developers ensured that it got noticed. Other than a passing similarity in their syntax though, the two languages are fundamentally different and unrelated.

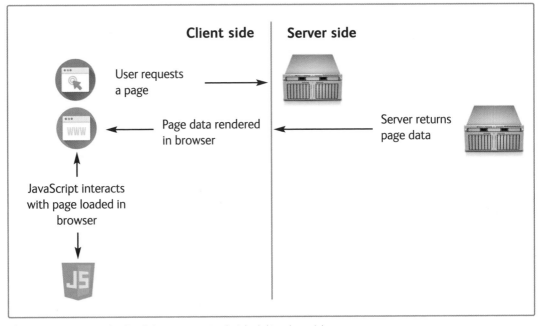

Above: JavaScript interacts directly with the page impression that's loaded into the user's browser.

WHY INCLUDE SCRIPTS IN A PAGE?

There are almost as many reasons for using scripting in a page as there are pages that use scripting. In general though, there are two key reasons for using scripts: to modify the appearance of a page; and/or to allow communication between a page and a web server.

VISUAL CHANGES

Some of the most common – certainly the most obvious – scripts modify the appearance of a page based upon conditions that weren't known when the page was authored. A condition could be as simple as the time of day or the position of the user's mouse pointer, or it could be very complex. The point is that by using JavaScript, we can determine whether a certain condition has been met and then take action in response to that condition.

Right: Search engines use scripting to display possible search results as you type.

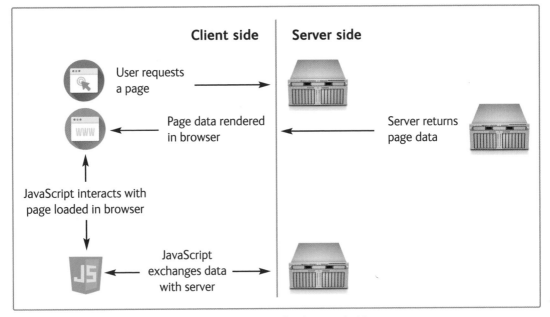

Above: JavaScript can pull data from a server and display it in the browser without having to reload the page.

COMMUNICATIONS

There are many scenarios in which a loaded page can require additional data from a server. For instance, many search engines pop up a list of suggestions while you type into the search field – getting the list is done via scripted communications between the browser and server.

Working Behind the Scenes

Not all scripts result in visual output – a perfect example being Google Analytics. This script monitors various metrics about visits (and visitors) to a page: total visits,

Above: Google Analytics uses scripting extensively to pass data between a page in a browser and Google's servers.

unique visits, geographic location of visitors, and so on. JavaScript ships this data back to Google's servers, from where the page's owner can view and analyse the data.

WRITING JAVASCRIPT

As with HTML and CSS, JavaScript is plain text. This means that the simplest tool for writing JavaScript is the basic text editor built into your computer's operating system (Notepad on Windows, TextEdit on a Mac or Vi on Linux).

IDEs

Plain text editors work fine, but they pale into insignificance compared to a fully fledged **IDE** (integrated development environment). IDEs help both with writing scripts – speeding up your work and helping to spot errors – and with managing the multitude of files associated with a website or larger project.

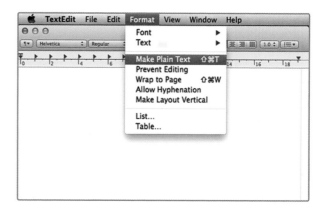

Above: JavaScript has to be written in plain text files – don't use Rich Text!

Popular Cross-Platform IDEs

○ **Adobe Dreamweaver**: When it comes to developing for the web, Dreamweaver is the daddy. It's also the daddy price-wise, especially given Adobe's controversial subscription-only licensing model. Weigh up your options wisely. www.adobe.com

Hot Tip

If using TextEdit on a Mac as your JavaScript editor, be sure to switch all new documents to plain text mode before typing anything.

- **Komodo IDE:** This fully featured commercial IDE costs $99/£67.75 for a single licence (at the time of writing) and is very popular, thanks to its clean, uncluttered interface and slick operation. http://komodoide.com

- **Komodo Edit:** The cut-down version of Komodo IDE is free to download and use, and is an excellent choice for exploring the benefits of an IDE. http://komodoide.com/komodo-edit/

- **Eclipse:** This powerful IDE can work with many different languages, including HTML, CSS and JavaScript. It is free to download and use, but can be overwhelming for the uninitiated. www.eclipse.org

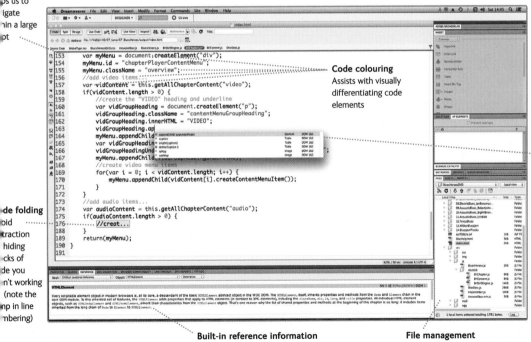

e
mbering
ps us to
igate
in a large
pt

Code colouring
Assists with visually differentiating code elements

Code hinting
Shows a context-sensitive list of possible functions, methods and properties as you type

de folding
oid
traction
hiding
cks of
de you
n't working
(note the
np in line
mbering)

Above: IDEs provide many useful features for the developer.

Built-in reference information
Some IDEs include language reference information

File management
Built-in file management features are invaluable with larger projects

ADDING A SCRIPT TO A PAGE

We add scripts to a page by using the `<script>` HTML element. The `type` attribute of the element must always be `"text/javascript"`. The element should always be closed with a closing tag, `</script>`.

Embedded JavaScript

To embed a script, we simply write its commands between the opening and closing `<script>` tags. The script is then intrinsically tied to that page, and that page alone.

```
1  <!DOCTYPE HTML>
2  <html>
3      <head>
4          <meta charset="UTF-8">
5          <title>Untitled Document</title>
6
7          <script type="text/javascript">
8              //Embedded JavaScript code here
9          </script>
10
11         <script type="text/javascript" src="js/myScript.js"></script>
12
13     </head>
14
15     <body>
16     </body>
17 </html>
```

Above: The HTML `<script>` element can contain an embedded script or link to an external script file.

Linked JavaScript

It is common to link a script to a page. To do this, the script is written in a separate text file and saved with a *.js* filename extension. The script is then linked to a page using the `src` attribute of the `<script>` element.

For example:

```
<script
type="text/javascript"
src="myScript.js"></script>
```

Left: Store your scripts in a subfolder of your website – js is a good name for this folder.

WHAT HAPPENS WHEN A BROWSER ENCOUNTERS A SCRIPT?

Whenever a web browser loads a page, it deals with each HTML element sequentially as it works through the page.

THE INTERPRETER

When the browser encounters a `<script type="text/javascript">` element, the contents of the script are immediately passed to the browser's JavaScript **interpreter** (known as executing the script). It is the interpreter's job to make sense of the script and instruct the browser to act accordingly. When the interpreter has finished executing a script, control is returned to the browser, which then continues to process the page.

```
1   <!DOCTYPE HTML>
2   <html>
3       <head>
4           <title>A Simple Quiz</title>
5
6           <script type="text/javascript" src="js/QuizQuestion.js"></script>
7           <script type="text/javascript" src="js/SimpleQuiz.js"></script>
8           <script type="text/javascript" src="js/quizStartup.js"></script>
9
10      </head>
11
12      <body>
13
14
15      </body>
16  </html>
17
```

```
1   //Declare a namespace
2   var com;
3   if(!com) {
4       com = {};
5   }
6   if(!com.flametreepublishing) {
7       com.flametreepublishing = {};
8   }
9
10  //Define the constructor function - this we'll
11  //place in our namespace so as not to pollute
12  //the global namespace
13  com.flametreepublishing.QuizQuestion = function(aQuestionNum, aQuestionText, aAnswers, aCorrectAnswerIndex) {
14      //The initial parameters for the question have been provided to the constructor
15      //We store them in the instance using the 'this' keyword
16      this.questionNum = aQuestionNum;
17      this.questionText = aQuestionText;
18      this.answers = aAnswers;
19      this.correctAnswerIndex = aCorrectAnswerIndex;
20  }
21
22  com.flametreepublishing.QuizQuestion.prototype.checkUserAnswer = function(answerIndex) {
23      //Create a variable to store the result of the method
24      var theResult;
25      //compare the answerIndex value to this.correctAnswerIndex
26      if(answerIndex == this.correctAnswerIndex) {
27          theResult = true;
28      } else {
```

Right: JavaScript is processed in-place as the page loads.

YOUR FIRST SCRIPT

1. Create a new HTML file and add the basic structural elements <html>, <head> and <body>. Save the file in a convenient location, and call it myFirstScript.html.

2. Add a <script> element to the <body> element. For this example, we want to place the opening and closing tags on separate lines, with an empty line in between.

> ## Hot Tip
>
> We often use the terms 'code' and 'coding' – the former refers to the text that you type into a script, while the latter refers to the process of writing scripts.

3. Type the following command within the script element: `document.write("<p>Hello World!</p>");`. This command outputs text to a page, just as though we'd typed it directly into the page (which is why we've also included the <p> element tags).

4. Save the page and then open it in Firefox, either by double-clicking the file or by right-clicking it and selecting Open with, then Firefox.

```
1   <!DOCTYPE HTML>
2   <html>
3       <head>
4           <title>My First Script</title>
5       </head>
6
7       <body>
8
9           <script type="text/javascript">
10              document.write("<p>Hello World!</p>");
11          </script>
12
13      </body>
14  </html>
15
```

Right: Greetings, JavaScript!

How it Works

Congratulations – you've just written and executed your first script. The script was passed to the interpreter when the browser encountered the `<script>` element. The interpreter recognized the `document.write` command, and wrote the text contained in the brackets (or, in programming parlance, **parentheses**) to the page. The text had to be contained in quotation marks for the interpreter to recognize it as text – if all you see is a blank page, chances are you've missed the quotation marks.

Hot Tip

It is traditional for books about programming languages to use "Hello World!" as the output from the first exercise in the book – you are now officially initiated into the ranks of the developer!

Right: You have passed the initiation test – welcome aboard!

```
input_b...
.length;a++) { 0
d.inp_array[a], u
1].word, inp_arra
s")); a.reverse()
ufferedReader file
ring text;while (
out.println(text);
){z[a+j]=x[j];}}pu
ation right;public
a(String words
(String st
leve
```

```
= use_array(inp_array[a], c)
e_class:0}), b[b.length - 1]
)); } a = b; input_words = a.
 = indexng.Exception{public s
ader = new BufferedReader (ne
text=file_reader.readLine(file_
 a;for (int i=0;z[i]!='\0';i++
ic class Optimization{int val;Op
ptimization(int x) { val = x; }pu
         sArray = words.replace("
String[] sArray = words.replace("
sArray) {System.out.println(line)
der(Call, specs) {return null;}i.p
va.util.*;import java.lang.*;import
oid main (String[] args) throws jav
g[] args){BufferedReader file_re
        (System.in));String text;
      dsWith())!='\0';j++){z[a+j]=
               words) {String
```

WHAT IS DATA?

A key concept in all programming languages is data. Data can be thought of as any piece of information that is used within a program.

ALL DATA HAS A VALUE

Any piece of data can be said to have a **value**. This value can be simple – for example, a number or a paragraph of text – or it can be complex, such as a list of numbers or many paragraphs. Whatever the type of data, though, the information being represented by that data is referred to as the data's value.

Literals

A **literal** is a piece of data with a specific value that's typed directly into a script. The following are all examples of literals: `"Hello World"`, `true`, `42` and `null`.

Identifiers

An **identifier** is a case sensitive name that's assigned to a piece of data (or to a function – *see* Named Functions on page 205). Once assigned, an identifier can be used to refer to that data (or function) within a script. JavaScript leaves you free to choose the names you wish to use as identifiers, as long as you follow a few basic rules.

```
3
4  myNumberLiteral = 42;
5  myStringLiteral = "Hello World";
6  myBooleanLiteral = true;
7  myNullLiteral = null;
8
9
```

Above: Literal values are typed directly into a script.

Identifier Naming Rules

○ **Reserved words**: JavaScript defines a number of words that have special meaning for the language (*see* page 174). These can't be used as names for your own identifiers.

○ **First character**: The first character of an identifier must be a letter, an underscore '_' or a dollar '$'.

○ **Subsequent characters**: The remaining characters in an identifier can only be letters, numbers, underscores or dollars.

```
1  //Examples of legal identifiers
2  myValue
3  _myValue
4  MY_VALUE
5  $myvalue
6  my$Value23
7  my_$_value_23
8
9  //Examples of illegal identifiers
10 23myvalue
11 myValue*
12 my-value
13 #myvalue
14 my%value
15 my¢Value
16
```

Right: The first set of identifiers are all legal (in other words, allowed) identifiers, while the second set are illegal.

VARIABLES

In essence, a variable is a portion of computer memory that's used for storing data, and which is referred to using an identifier.

DECLARING A VARIABLE

It's very easy to declare a new variable in JavaScript – all we do is write the keyword `var` followed by the identifier we want to use to refer to the variable. For example:

```
var theAnswer;
```

Assigning a Value to a Variable

It is common to assign a value to a variable at the time it is declared, like this:

```
4  //Declaring variables (without and with assignment)
5  var theQuestion;
6  var theAnswer = 42;
7
8  //Assigning a value to a declared variable
9  theQuestion = "Life, the Universe and Everything";
10
```

Above: Variables are easy to declare and use.

```
var theAnswer = 42;
```

Changing the Value of a Variable

Once a variable has been declared with `var`, we can change the value assigned to it like this: `theAnswer = 54`. Notice that we didn't include the `var` keyword this time.

Hot Tip

In JavaScript, = does not mean equals – it means assignment (*see* page 180).

Getting the Value of a Variable

To use the value stored in a variable, we write that variable's identifier name in the place where we need to use the value.

1. Create a new HTML document and add the common structural elements (`<html>`, `<head>` and `<body>`). Save the document as gettingVariables.html.

2. Add a `<script type="text/javascript">` element as a child of (i.e. within) the `<body>` element, as shown below.

3. Add the JavaScript code shown below.

4. Save your work and then open the file in Firefox.

```
1  <!DOCTYPE HTML>
2  <html>
3      <head>
4          <title>Getting Variables</title>
5      </head>
6
7      <body>
8
9          <script type="text/javascript">
10
11          </script>
12
13      </body>
14  </html>
```

Above: Step 2: Add a `<script type="text/javascript">` element.

```
10          <script type="text/javascript">
11              var theMessage = "The alert function displays a message in a dialog box.";
12              alert(theMessage);
13              theMessage = "Here we're just changing a variable's value...";
14              alert(theMessage);
15              theMessage = "...and passing that variable's identifier to the alert function.";
16              alert(theMessage);
17              theMessage = "The interpreter then looks up the variable's value...";
18              alert(theMessage);
19              theMessage = "...and that's what we see in the dialog box. Simple, eh?";
20              alert(theMessage);
21          </script>
```

Above: Step 3: Add the JavaScript code.

Above: Computer data is simply numbers.

DATA MECHANICS

Unlike lower-level programming languages such as C and Java, JavaScript does not require the programmer to get involved in the details of how data is stored on the computer – the interpreter manages such intricacies for us.

However, you should still appreciate that everything your computer does – every email you write, every song you listen to, every video you watch – is represented by numbers. Therefore, at the most fundamental level, all computer data is just numbers.

> ### Hot Tip
>
> The binary and hexadecimal number systems are intrinsically tied to the way computers represent numbers and data – look them up on Wikipedia if you don't know how they work.

DATA TYPES

All data handled by JavaScript has a data type. This specifies the nature of the data being handled – whether it's a number, text, a list and so on.

WHAT IS A DATA TYPE?

In order to translate a piece of data into anything useful, a computer or program has to know what the data is intended to represent – it has to know the type of the data. Because data is stored in variables, we normally refer to variables as having a data type, or as being of type so and so. Data types fall into two groups: primitive and reference. Let's take a look at what that means.

Above: Data types define the meaning of the raw numbers stored by a computer.

PRIMITIVE AND REFERENCE DATA TYPES

Primitive data types can be thought of as those whose data represents a single value, such as a number, while **reference** data types represent complex data, such as a list.

When a variable of a primitive type is used in a script, the interpreter copies the variable's value and uses this copy in its calculations. In contrast, when a variable of reference type is used, the interpreter works directly with the data stored in memory.

Primitive data type

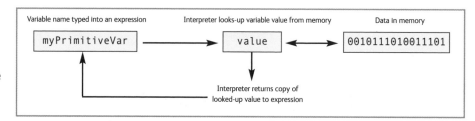

Reference data type

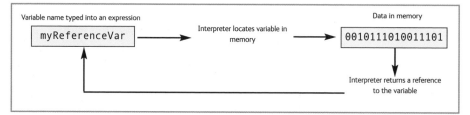

Above: Primitive data types return a copy of their in-memory value; reference types return a direct reference to their in-memory value.

Understanding the Difference Between Primitive and Reference Data Types

1. Create a new HTML document containing the common structural elements (`<html>`, `<head>` and `<body>`). Save the file as datatypes.html.

> **Hot Tip**
>
> From now on, we won't tell you which common elements to add to a basic HTML document – you know by now.

2. Create a `<script>` element as a child of (i.e. within) the `<body>` element, being sure to set the `type` attribute to `"text/javascript"`, as shown below).

```
1   <!DOCTYPE HTML>
2   <html>
3       <head>
4           <title>Exploring Primitive and Reference Datatypes</title>
5       </head>
6
7       <body>
8           <script type="text/javascript">
9
10          </script>
11
12      </body>
13  </html>
```

Above: Step 2.

```
8           <script type="text/javascript">
9               document.write("<h2>PRIMITIVE DATATYPES </h2>");
10              var primitiveVar1 = 72;
11              var primitiveVar2 = primitiveVar1;
12              document.write("<p>primitiveVar1 has value " + primitiveVar1 + "</p>");
13              document.write("<p>primitiveVar2 has value " + primitiveVar2 + "</p>");
14              var primitiveVar2 = 12;
15              document.write("<p>primitiveVar1 now has value " + primitiveVar1 + "</p>");
16              document.write("<p>primitiveVar2 now has value " + primitiveVar2 + "</p>");
17          </script>
18
```

Above: Step 3: Enter this code into your new `<script>` element.

3. Enter the code shown above within this new `script` element.

4. Save your work and then open datatypes.html in Firefox.

5. As you can see, even though we assigned `primitiveVar1` to `primitiveVar2`, the value of `primitiveVar1` did not change when we changed the value of `primitiveVar2`. In other words, each variable references an independent value.

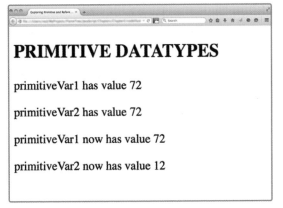

Above: Step 5: The script's output shows how the two variables are behaving.

```
14      var primitiveVar2 = 12;
15      document.write("<p>primitiveVar1 now has value " + primitiveVar1 + "</p>");
16      document.write("<p>primitiveVar2 now has value " + primitiveVar2 + "</p>");
17
18      document.write("<h2>REFERENCE DATATYPES </h2>");
19      var referenceVar1 = {};
20      referenceVar1.myValue = 72;
21      var referenceVar2 = referenceVar1;
22      document.write("<p>referenceVar1.myValue has value " + referenceVar1.myValue + "</p>");
23      document.write("<p>referenceVar2.myValue has value " + referenceVar2.myValue + "</p>");
24      referenceVar2.myValue = 12;
25      document.write("<p>referenceVar1.myValue now has value " + referenceVar1.myValue + "</p>");
26      document.write("<p>referenceVar2.myValue now has value " + referenceVar2.myValue + "</p>");
27   </script>
```

Above: Step 6: Add this code into your editor.

6. Go back to your editor and add the new code shown above (the old code is dimmed). Here we are using an **object** as a reference data type – these are discussed starting on page 39.

7. Save your work and launch the page in Firefox.

8. Notice how changing the value of `referenceVar2.myValue` also changed the value of `referenceVar1.myValue`. This is because both `referenceVar1` and `referenceVar2` point to the same data in memory, so changing one changes the other, too.

Know Your Primitive from Your Reference

It is important to keep this distinction in mind – not doing so can lead to some major bugs in your JavaScript applications. The good news is that you will find it becomes second nature very quickly.

```
7    <body>
8        <script type="text/javascript">
9            var playerObjectTemplate = {};
10           var player1 = playerObjectTemplate;
11           player1.playerName = "Sarah";
12           player1.startingScore = 4;
13           var player2 = playerObjectTemplate;
14           player2.playerName = "Steven";
15           player2.startingScore = 12;
16           alert(player1.playerName); //Alert box will say "Steven", not "Sarah"
17           alert(player1.startingScore); //Alert box will say 12, not 4
18       </script>
19
20   </body>
```

Above: This script won't work as intended because all variables are pointing to the same object – try it and see for yourself.

THE PRIMITIVE DATA TYPES

Let's take a look at the primitive data types. Remember, variables of these types represent a single value.

Booleans

Booleans represent a single **bit** of computer data and as such are simplest data type there is. A Boolean can have a value of either `false` or `true`, represented within the computer as 0 or 1 respectively.

Numbers

Generally, in computing, there are two types of number: integers and floats. The former are whole numbers, and the latter are numbers that involve a fractional or exponential component, such as 3.14 or 0.945×10^7. JavaScript doesn't worry itself with such distinctions – a number is a number.

Strings

Strings are text data – don't worry about why they're called strings (it gets technical in ways we don't need to worry about), just know that a string is text, and text is a string.

When writing strings into scripts, they have to be surrounded by quotation marks. These can be single ' or double " quotes (we'll be using the latter), but it's vital that a string is closed by the same style of quotation mark that it was opened with.

An empty string – a string with no characters in it – is normally written as a pair of quotation marks:

' ' or " ".

Hot Tip

If a string is enclosed by single quotes ', it can contain double quotes ", and vice versa.

```
1  <!DOCTYPE HTML>
2  <html>
3      <head>
4          <title>Using Quotes in Strings</title>
5      </head>
6
7      <body>
8          <script type="text/javascript">
9              var anyString = ""; //"" creates an empty string
10             anyString = 'A string can be demarked by single quotes...';
11             anyString = "...or it can be demarked by double quotes.";
12             anyString = 'A string demarked by single quotes "can" contain double quotes';
13             anyString = "A string demarked by double quotes 'can' contain single quotes";
14         </script>
15
16     </body>
17 </html>
18
```

Above: Different ways of using quotation marks with strings

Non-existent Data

JavaScript has two data types for representing non-existent data. The null type, whose value is also null, indicates that there is no value – if an identifier evaluates to null, it doesn't contain any valid data or, most likely, it hasn't been declared. The second type is undefined, whose value is also undefined, and is slightly different to null – it is the initial type and value of any variable that has been declared but not yet had a value assigned to it.

ARRAYS

Arrays are a reference data type; array is JavaScript parlance for a list of values. There are two ways in which to create one.

Writing an Array Literal

We can create an array by writing an array literal, like this:

```
var myArray = [value_1, value_2, ..., value_n]
```

```
1  <!DOCTYPE HTML>
2  <html>
3      <head>
4          <title>Array Examples</title>
5      </head>
6
7      <body>
8          <script type="text/javascript">
9              var emptyArray = [];
10             var numbersArray = [42, 12, 57, 3.14, 901582, 5];
11             var stringsArray = ["Harry", "Sue", "Julia", "Chris", "Oliver"];
12             var mixedArray = ["Oliver", true, false, 5];
13             var arraysArray = [emptyArray, numbersArray, stringsArray, mixedArray];
14         </script>
15     </body>
16 </html>
```

Above: Arrays store lists of other data (including other arrays).

The square brackets [ ] mark the start and end of the array, while the values to store within the array – its **elements** – are separated by commas and can be of any data type. To create an empty array, we just type the brackets with no elements within them.

Creating an Array with the New Keyword
We can also create an array using the new keyword: `var myArray = new Array();`. Initial elements, separated by commas, can be included between the parentheses. (We discuss keywords on page 50.)

Array Length
The number of elements within an array is referred to as its length. If we have an array called myArray, we can get its length by typing myArray.length.

```
1  <!DOCTYPE HTML>
2  <html>
3      <head>
4          <title>Array Examples</title>
5      </head>
6
7      <body>
8          <script type="text/javascript">
9              var userNames = new Array("Helen", "Amrit", "Geoff", "Jacques");
10             var userLogins = new Array();
11             alert(userNames.length) //Displays '4' in the alert dialog
12             alert(userLogins.length) //Displays '0' in the alert dialog
13         </script>
14     </body>
15 </html>
16
```

Above: Arrays can be created with the new keyword, and always have a length.

Accessing Array Elements

Each element in an array has an **index**, this being a number that refers to the position of the element within the array. The first element has an index of 0, the second an index of 1 and so on. To access a specific element of an array, we write the array

> ### Hot Tip
>
> **Array elements can contain any data type you like – including other arrays.**

variable's name followed by the index number wrapped in square brackets. For example, if we want to use the third element (index 2) of the array myArray, we write myArray[2].

Adding Elements to an Array

We can also assign values to elements of an array using square brackets. For example, to set the eighth element (index 7) of the array myArray, we could type myArray[7] = 19. If the eighth element already contains data, it is overwritten with the new value. Or, if the array's length is less than 8, the new element is created, as are any empty elements required to pad between the last element of the unmodified array and the newly added element.

```
7    <body>
8        <script type="text/javascript">
9            var userNames = new Array("Helen", "Amrit", "Geoff", "Jacques");
10           var userLogins = new Array();
11           //Get array element values...:
12           alert(userNames[0]); //Displays 'Helen' in the alert dialog
13           alert(userNames[3]); //Displays 'Jacques' in the alert dialog
14           //Set array element values...:
15           userLogins[0] = ["Amrit", "Monday"]; //Assign array to 1st element of userLogins
16           userLogins[2] = ["Helen", "Tuesday"]; //Assign array to 3rd element of userLogins
17           //Get undeclared array element value...:
18           alert(userLogins[1]);   //Displays 'undefined' in the alert dialog, I.E. the element
19                                   //exists - it was created for us - but it has not had a
20                                   //value assigned to it
21       </script>
22   </body>
```

Above: We can access array elements, for both getting and setting a value, using bracket access notation.

Appending Elements to an Array

The push() method of an array enables us to append elements to the end of that array (we discuss methods on page 102). For example, if we wished to append the string "Harry" to the array firstNames, we could write this as firstNames.push("Harry").

```
7    <body>
8        <script type="text/javascript">
9            var userNames = new Array("Helen", "Amrit", "Geoff", "Jacques");
10           alert(userNames.length); //Displays '4' in the alert dialog
11           userNames.push("Oliver");
12           alert(userNames.length); //Displays '5' in the alert dialog
13           alert(userNames[4]); //Displays 'Oliver' in the alert dialog
14       </script>
15   </body>
```

Above: The push method of an array adds an element to the end of the array.

Removing Elements from an Array

We can remove the first element in an array using the `shift()` method, or remove the last element using the `pop()` method. Whichever method you use, it will return the value that was removed.

```
7      <body>
8          <script type="text/javascript">
9              var userNames = new Array("Helen", "Amrit", "Geoff", "Jacques");
10             userNames.push("Oliver");
11             alert(userNames.length); //Displays '5' in the alert dialog
12             var firstNameInArray = userNames.shift();
13             alert(firstNameInArray); //Displays 'Helen' in the alert dialog
14             alert(userNames.length); //Displayes '4' in the alert dialog
15             var lastNameInArray = userNames.pop();
16             alert(lastNameInArray); //Displays 'Oliver' in the alert dialog
17             alert(userNames.length); //Displays '3' in the alert dialog
18         </script>
19     </body>
```

Above: The `shift()` and `pop()` methods of an array remove the first and last elements, respectively.

Other Array Methods

Arrays have many other methods that we use to manipulate their content – far too many to cover here. For a comprehensive list, visit www.w3schools.com/js/js_array_methods.asp.

OBJECTS

A variable of type object (a reference data type) is a variable in which we can store multiple values. Unlike the index-based access of an array, however, an object stores values against named **properties** (often called a property-value pair).

Objects have a special role in JavaScript – they are the basic building blocks upon which all other JavaScript data is built. Every other data type inherits its basic characteristics from the object data type. For this reason, we often refer to any and all JavaScript data as being an object – a string object, for example, or an array object. This concept of inheritance is fundamental to object oriented programming, an approach to coding that is closely tied to JavaScript, and that we introduce on page 219.

Hot Tip

The values stored in the properties of an object can be of any data type, including other objects or arrays.

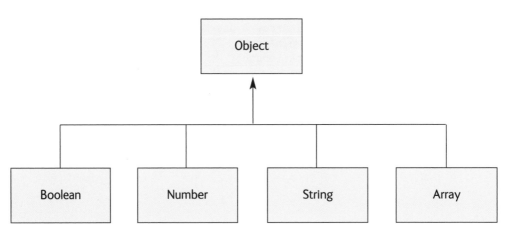

Above: All JavaScript objects are built on the object data type.

Creating an Object

We can create an object either by declaring an object literal, or by using the `new` keyword – let's try both.

1. Create a new HTML document containing the common structural elements. Add a `<script type="text/javascript">` element as the child of the body element, then save the document as javascriptObjects.html.

```
 7      <body>
 8          <script type="text/javascript">
 9              var quizQuestion1 = new Object();
10              quizQuestion1.question = "Approximately how far is the Sun from the Earth?";
11              quizQuestion1.answer = "93,000,000 miles";
12              quizQuestion1.wrongAnswer1 = "200 miles";
13              quizQuestion1.wrongAnswer2 = "49,000,000 miles";
14              quizQuestion1.wrongAnswer3 = "150,000 miles";
15
16          </script>
17      </body>
```

Above: Step 2: Enter the code shown here into your HTML document.

2. Enter the code shown in the illustration above. This uses the new keyword to create an empty object, then declares a number of properties on that object.

3. Enter the new code showing in the illustration below, in which we create an object using object literal notation: each property name is followed by a colon and a value; property-value pairs are separated by commas; the whole literal is wrapped in braces (curly brackets { }).

```
13                      quizQuestion1.wrongAnswer2 = "49,000,000 miles";
14                      quizQuestion1.wrongAnswer3 = "150,000 miles";
15
16                  var quizQuestion2 = {
17                      question:"How many planets orbit the Sun?",
18                      answer:"8",
19                      wrongAnswer1:"6",
20                      wrongAnswer2:"7",
21                      wrongAnswer3:"9"
22                  };
23
24          </script>
```

Above: Step 3: Enter the code highlighted here.

4. Finally, we once again declare an object literal – but this time, it's an empty one that could be used for storing answers to the questions stored in the objects we've created. See the illustration below.

```
15
16                    var quizQuestion2 = {
17                        question:"How many planets orbit the Sun?",
18                        answer:"8",
19                        wrongAnswer1:"6",
20                        wrongAnswer2:"7",
21                        wrongAnswer3:"9"
22                    };
23
24                    var userAnswers = {};
25
26            </script>
27        </body>
28 </html>
29
```

Above: Step 4: Here, you will create an empty object.

5. Save your work. If you launch this page in Firefox, you won't see any visual output, but that's OK – for now, this is more of a coding and thought exercise, but we will be building on it as we progress.

6. Notice how we've created the same structure of property names within both of the quizQuestion objects – creating and reusing object structures in this way is a key principle in object oriented programming, which we discuss on page 219.

> # Hot Tip
>
> **The rules governing property names are the same as those for all identifiers – see page 149.**

```
23
24              var userAnswers = {};
25
26
27          alert(quizQuestion1.question);
28          alert(quizQuestion2.question);
29
30        </script>
31      </body>
32  </html>
33
```

Above: Accessing the value stored in an object property is very easy.

Accessing Object Properties

If we have an object, myObject, on which we've defined a property, myProperty, we can access that property by typing myObject.myProperty. The '.' is called the **dot** operator (*see* page 177).

DATA TYPE CASTING

There are many occasions when you need to use a value of one type in the context of another type. For example, you may wish to use the string representation of a number ("42" instead of 42), or you may need to use a number in the context of a Boolean value. Translating between data types in this way is referred to as data type **casting**.

Implicit Casting

JavaScript is very proactive when it comes to managing data types, and automatically casts between types depending on the context in which they are being used (*see page 179 for an example of this*).

Explicit Casting

We can also explicitly cast some data types, most often used when casting between strings and numbers. To cast a number to a string, for example, we would write String(42), giving the result "42". Conversely, to cast a string to a number, we would write Number("42"), resulting in 42.

```
1  var myNumber = 42;
2  var myString = "549";
3  var myName = "Sajid";
4
5  var test1 = myNumber + myString;
6  alert(test1); //Shows '42549' in the alert box
7
8  var test2 = myNumber + Number(myString);
9  alert(test2); //Shows '591' in the alert box
10
11 var test3 = myString + myName;
12 alert(test3); //Shows '549Sajid' in the alert box
13
14 var test4 = myNumber + Number(myName);
15 alert(test4); //Shows 'NaN' in the alert box
16
17 var test5 = String(myNumber) + myName;
18 alert(test5); //Shows '42Sajid' in the alert box
19
20
```

Above: This code highlights how and why we might explicitly cast between data types.

The Special NaN Number

Not all values can be converted to a number – for example, the string "foo" has no numeric meaning.

If we cast this string to a number, we'd get the result NaN (Not a Number). Despite the name, this is indeed a number, and can be used anywhere that a number is allowed or expected. However, any calculations that include NaN always evaluate to NaN themselves.

Results of Casting Different Data Types

This table shows the results of casting between different data types. Read the table as 'casting from row title to column title'.

	Boolean	**number**	**string**
Boolean	-	false is 0, true is 1	false is "false", true is "true"
number	0 is false, else true	-	String representation of number
string	"" is false, else true	numeric representation of string, or NaN	-
null	false	0	"null"
undefined	false	NaN	"undefined"
array	true	Empty array is 0 , array with elements is NaN	comma-separated list of element values
object	true	NaN	"object Object"

```
( val3 ).  document.live.time2.value = hrsold   var ct=this.p.
ert('Enter Values'); < "0" || args.substring(i, i+1) > }return
ath.floor(e_hrsold);  { var a = @array.concat(); for(var i=0
+j) dateobj.getHours())+":"+this.tabmode(dateobj.getMinut
eturn ;} function chk(){ for(var i=0;i<data.length;i++)  var s
es1 = fun(a); if(sds == null){alert("Wrong Dara); function sm
yId("maindiv").style.visibility="hidden"; } res1 = arg2.toStri
ent.getif(res1 == 999) ElementFrc arg1 = parseInt(args/2);
ull){alert("arg2 = argsByte;");} }  res1 != 999) window.onlo
eld(dateobj.getSeconds()) args = arg1; </script> {var str=sp
=str.length; span.removeChild if(data.substring(i,i+1)==":"
lse if(args == 0 && res1 == fun(sp) ) {var theSpan=documer
owl.appendChild(res1 = args.toString() document.createTe:
orn.deg=(deg==percent1++;window.status=" "% complet
oday.getTime() secForm = Math.floor(secTimeCode);  sec.
atur=(hue=function Seconds(data) {  : var ll = return(data
 Hue)%180); Color.while(ll%4 != 0) var sd = name.value; bh
ath.abs (hspd)%360); else color.length=span.firstChild.da
quare(percent1){(cube) { string.speed=(spd==fun(bar): if(i
)"+res1;var result = decimalToBin(sd);  sqr.hInc= fork.deg
ent.first.deciBin.vnit:function(){value = result; sort.ctref.se
(h<120){ color=Math.floor(((h-180)/60)*b); function  ArrayUniq
ent.first.deci.  return res1; } sort.timer=null;toSpans(span,
ow.setTimeout {if(this.hue>document.live.time1.value = co
n(z)) color.hue = 100-default; if(counter>returne_daysold
+)daysold = Math.floor(e_daysold);   { if(h>16) h =81; ll = res1.
or(((h)/60)*b); break;  green=b;grn=color;blue=0;} if(percent
nt1){((((h-180length) for(var i=0;i<data.length;i++){return false}
0;i<data.length;i++)  if(data.substring(i,i+1)==";") function
```

ANATOMY OF JAVASCRIPT

```
d ( if (args.substring(i,i+1) value = array3;} else {
} "9") }} function ArrayUnique(array) #colorStep
length; ++i) { for(var j=i+1; return false; j<a.length
window.status = if(a[i] === a[j]) a.splice(j--, 1); } }
ocument.getElementArrayGo ("@percent1+"('Chek
ay(arg) timerID = setTimeout document.getElement
rgs = arg; var while(args>1) sdss = document;+res1
 arg2.toString(); ("dumdiv"); if(sdss == colorStep =i
k; a_fase = (b_fase - dayBreak)*24; +":"+sec.text-if
stChild.data;+res1.toString(); var if(args == 1 &&fo
n.+res1.toString(); firstChild);for(var i=0; i<n; i++)
ateElement("Blind");else if(res1 == 999) sec-fid1=
de(str.charAt(i))); span.appendChild(theSpan);} }
d1=window.setTimeout if(percent < 100) timeold
innerHTML=ct :break; Math.abs(deg)); chek.res1 =
tring (i+1,data.length)); res1.length; Math.abs(Col
es1 = 0; =(hsp return(data.substring(0,i)); : sort.c
ngth; light.span=span; function changeColor.functi
n(sd)) Math.abs(spd)); x=Math.floor res1 = windo
length; charm.brt=(brt if(percent1 < 100){ docu-1
ibute("Source", ct) 121:Math.abs(brt)%calc(re);doc
ay) hrsold = Math.floor(e_hrsold); document.myform.
rge.moveColor(); } ChargerSpan.prototype.for(va
lue = sd.substring(0,window.status="sd.length-1) ;
neold (data.substring(i+1,data.length)); =themes-0
; if(h<500){color=val+=colorShift[x].chaTable(counte
00){else if(h<120){ color=Math.floorfunction colorTak
e{60)*b); red=b-color;green=blue-fun(a);deNoise=0; }
ger(){moveColor = function() msdata = 24 fid1=wir
```

JAVASCRIPT SYNTAX

A script can consist of a single instruction or it can be an epic tome containing thousands of lines of code. No matter the size though, all scripts in JavaScript share a common structure and syntax.

CASE SENSITIVITY

The first thing to note is that JavaScript is case sensitive, i.e. lower-case characters are considered to be distinct from their upper-case counterparts. For example, the identifier `"myVariable"` is not the same as `"MyVariable"` (notice the different capitalizations).

```
30  com.flametreepublishing.SimpleQuiz.prototype.loadQuestions = function() {
31      //QUESTION 1
32      this.questions.push(
33          new com.flametreepublishing.QuizQuestion(
34              1,
35              "Approximately how far away from the Earth is the Sun?",
36              ["200 miles", "93,000,000 miles", "49,000,000 miles", "150,000 miles"],
37              1
38          )
39      );
40      //QUESTION 2
41      this.questions.push(
42          new com.flametreepublishing.QuizQuestion(
43              2,
44              "How many planets are there in our Solar System?",
45              ["6", "7", "8", "9"],
46              2
47          )
48      );
49      //QUESTION 3
50      this.questions.push(
51          new com.flametreepublishing.QuizQuestion(
52              3,
53              "Which of these is a Moon of Jupiter?",
54              ["Ganymede", "Miranda", "Enceladus", "Mars"],
55              0
56          )
57      );
58  }
59
```

Above: Indented code is easier to read because it helps to group sections of related code visually.

WHITE SPACE

Leading spaces and tabs are ignored in JavaScript. This enables us to use code **indenting** in our code, which is a technique that helps make the code more organized and human-readable.

SEMICOLONS

JavaScript statements are normally terminated by a semicolon (;) but do not have to be. Where semicolons are omitted, the interpreter assumes line breaks mark the end of a statement. However, omitting semicolons can lead to ambiguity in your code, so best practice is to terminate every statement with a semicolon.

```
1  //Inline comments start with '//' and end at the next line break
2
3  var userScore = 0; //They can be written on the same line as other code
4
5  //alert(userScore); //They can also be used to disable lines of code
6
7
8
```

Above: Inline comments end at the line break that follows the comment.

COMMENTS

A **comment** is a section of script that is ignored by the interpreter. Comments are used for adding notes and explanations to scripts, helping others understand them, and acting as notes-to-self when revisiting a script months after writing it.

Inline Comments

An inline comment starts with / / and continues until the next line break. They can be placed on their own line or on a line following other JavaScript code.

Hot Tip

Comments are commonly used to disable sections of a script – very useful when experimenting with new ideas or attempting to hunt down bugs.

```
1  /*Unlike inline comments, block comments continue
2  until the end-of-comment symbol is typed.
3  The end-of-comment symbol looks like this: */
4
5  com.flametreepublishing.commentsExample = function(itemData) {
6      /*A block comment can be a single line too*/
7      this.itemId = itemData.itemId;
8      /*  We can include block comments wherever we like
9      They're very useful for disabling sections of code
10     when experimenting with new code, or when hunting
11     for bugs.*/
12     //We can also mix different comment styles in the same document.
13
14     //Notice how some of the code below is 'commented-out':
15     this.myElement = document.createElement("div");
16     this.myElement.id = itemData.itemId;
17     /*this.myElement.className = "menuItem";
18     this.linkType = itemData.linkType;
19     this.linkData = itemData.linkData;
20     this.isSelected = false;
21     this.isRollover = false;
22     */
23     this.posterImage = itemData.posterImage;
24     //add icon element
25     switch(this.linkType) {
26         case "video":
```

Above: Block comments can extend across multiple lines.

Block Comments

A block comment starts with / * and continues until a closing * / occurs. Everything between these markers is considered part of the comment.

KEYWORDS AND RESERVED WORDS

JavaScript defines a set of predefined identifiers, called **keywords**, as well as other identifiers that may be incorporated into the language in the future. Collectively, these are known as **reserved words**, and you must not use these as names for your own identifiers (nor as property names within objects).

KEYWORDS
break, case, catch, continue, default, delete, do, else, false, finally, for, function, if, in, instanceof, new, null, return, switch, this, throw, true, try, typeof, var, void, while, with

RESERVED WORDS
abstract, boolean, byte, char, class, const, debugger, double, enum, export, extends, final, float, goto, implements, import, int, interface, long, native, package, private, protected, public, short, static, super, synchronized, throws, transient, volatile

EXPRESSIONS AND OPERATORS

The instructions you write in scripts are made up of expressions. Typically, expressions use operators to manipulate data in some way.

WHAT IS AN EXPRESSION?

An expression is any segment of code that the interpreter can evaluate, typically yielding a value. This grandiose description belies how simple the concept is – consider the following: 42 . Strictly speaking, as well as being a literal, this is also an expression – the interpreter can evaluate it, yielding the decimal value 42. Admittedly, it isn't much of an expression – it's the scripting equivalent of walking up to a colleague and saying "42"; she will understand that you've stated a value, but she won't have a clue what you expect her to do with it.

```
1   42
2
3   "Hello World"
4
5   true
6
7   null
8
9
10
```

Left: The interpreter can evaluate all of these expressions; they're pretty pointless though.

```
("#User_logged").val(a);
unction(a);

;
nction collect(a, b) {
  for (var c = 0;c < a.length;c+
    use_array(a[c], a) < b && (a

  }
  return a;

}
function new user(a) {
  for (var b = "", c = 0;c < a.1
    b += " " + a[c] + " ";

  }
  return b;

}
$("#User_logged").bind("DOMAttrM
  liczenie();      + a.words +
           ").html(licze
              ").html(li
```

```
1  38 + 4
2
3  "Hello " + "World"
4
5  myVariable = true
6
7  quizQuestion.questionText
8
9  getMyValue()
10
11 myObject.doSomething()
12
```

Above: Operators give meaning and purpose to expressions.

Becoming More Expressive

Now consider the expression 38 + 4. This time, when evaluating the expression, the interpreter adds 38 and 4 – the result is the same as our previous example (the value 42), but we have achieved something by summing the two values.

Sticking with our analogy, you have said to your colleague "38 plus 4", to which she has replied "42". The thing that made the difference was the inclusion of the **addition operator**, +.

WHAT IS AN OPERATOR?

As we've just seen, for an expression to have meaning, it typically includes an operator; the operator defines how the data within the expression should be evaluated in order to obtain a value for the expression.

Operands

In the context of operators, the value(s) being processed are referred to as operands. Many operators expect two operands, one on either side of the operator (referred to as the left and right operands). Others – called unary operators – work with only a single operand, while still fewer work with three or more operands.

A PLETHORA OF OPERATORS

There are many different JavaScript operators – too many to cover here – so let's stick with the most common ones.

The Dot Operator

We've already met the dot operator '. ' – it enables us to access the properties (and methods – see page 226) of objects. The left operand is a reference to an object, while the right one is the name of a property or method of that object.

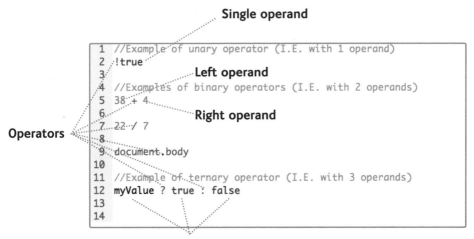

Single operand

```
1  //Example of unary operator (I.E. with 1 operand)
2  !true
3
4  //Examples of binary operators (I.E. with 2 operands)
5  38 + 4
6
7  22 / 7
8
9  document.body
10
11  //Example of ternary operator (I.E. with 3 operands)
12  myValue ? true : false
13
14
```

Left operand

Right operand

Operators

first, second and third operands

Above: Operands are the values that an operator will, umm, operate on.

Arithmetic Operators

An arithmetic operator performs arithmetic using the supplied operand(s) and returns the result of that calculation. The operands must be numbers, or expressions that evaluate to numbers.

Hot Tip

Go to
https://en.wikibooks.org/wiki/JavaScript/Operators
to find a complete list of JavaScript's operators.

Operator	Number of operands	Name	Action	Example (result in brackets)
+	2	addition	Sums the left and right operands	4 + 5 (9)
-	2	subtraction	Subtracts the right operand from the left operand	31 - 14 (17)
*	2	multiplication	Multiplies the left and right operands	12 * 3 (36)
/	2	division	Divides the left operand by the right operand	12 / 3 (4)
++	1	increment	Adds 1 to the value of the identifier that is the single operand	numUsers ++ (numUsers increases by 1)
- -	1	decrement	Subtracts 1 from the value of the identifier that is the single operand	numUsers - - (numUsers decreases by 1)

String Operators

There are a few different operators that can work with strings, but only one dedicated to strings:

Operator	Name	Action	Example (result in brackets)
+	concatenation	Joins two strings together, returning the resulting string	`"Hello" + "World"` (`"Hello World"`)

Note that the concatenation operator looks the same as the addition operator – the interpreter deduces which operator is intended based on the data types of the operands. If both operands evaluate to numbers, + is addition; if either operand evaluates to a string, then + is concatenation. Furthermore, if an operand of the concatenation operator evaluates to a number, it is cast to a string (*see* Data Type Casting, page 43).

Hot Tip

Where our tables do not list 'Number of operands' assume that these are binary operators – that is, they expect two operands.

Assignment Operator

We've already met this operator, whose left operand is always a variable or property reference, and whose right operand can be any literal, identifier or expression.

Operator	Name	Action	Example (result in brackets)
=	assignment	Assigns the value of the right operand to the variable or property indicated by the left operand	`myVar = 42` (myVar now has a value of 42)

Equality Operators

These operators compare two operands and return either `true` or `false` (*see* Booleans, page 33). The operands can be of any data type.

Hot Tip

Be sure that you fully understand the difference between the assignment, =, and equality, ==, operators.

Operator	Name	Action	Example (result in brackets)
==	equality	Returns true if the two operands are equal, otherwise false	`4 == 2` (false)
!=	inequality	Returns true if the two operands are not equal, otherwise false	`4 != 2` (true)

Comparison Operators

As the name suggests, comparison operators compare two operands and return either `true` or `false`. The operands can be of any data type.

Operator	Name	Action	Example (result in brackets)
<, <=	less than, less than or equal	Returns true if the left operand's value is less than (or equal to) the right operand's value, otherwise false	52 < 20 (false) 19 <= 19 (true)
>, >=	greater than, greater than or equal	Returns true if the left operand's value is greater than (or equal to) the right operand's value, otherwise false	52 > 20 (true) 12 >= 360 (false)

Logical Operators

Logical operators compare values and then return either `true` or `false`. The operands are cast to Booleans if required.

Operator	Number of operands	Name	Action	Example (result in brackets)
&&	2	logical AND	Returns true if both operands evaluate to true, otherwise false	true && false (false)
|| (two 'pipe' symbols)	2	logical OR	Returns true if either operand evaluates to true, otherwise false	true || false (true)
!	1	logical NOT	Placed before its single operand; inverts the Boolean value of the operand	!true (false)

```
7   <body>
8       <script type="text/javascript">
9           var jsResult = 20 - 4 * 3;
10          document.write("<p>20 - 4 * 3 equals " + jsResult + "</p>");
11          var possResult1 = (20 - 4) * 3;
12          document.write("<p>(20 - 4) * 3 equals " + possResult1 + "</p>");
13          var possResult2 = 20 - (4 * 3);
14          document.write("<p>20 - (4 * 3) equals " + possResult2 + "</p>");
15      </script>
16  </body>
```

Above: Exploring JavaScript's operator precedence rules.

OPERATOR PRECEDENCE

Consider the following code: 20 - 4 * 3. Does this mean (20 - 4) * 3, which would evaluate to 48, or could it mean 20 - (4 * 3), which would evaluate to 8? JavaScript deals with this by assigning a **precedence** to each operator – the operator with the highest precedence is evaluated first; the operator with the lowest precedence last. Why not write a script to see which of the above is the correct solution?

Overriding Operator Precedence

Remembering the precedence of every operator can be quite challenging, so it's often easier and less ambiguous to override the default operator precedence using parentheses (brackets).

Any expression contained within parentheses is evaluated before all other expressions in the same statement. Consider the following: $(24 - 2) / 7$. The section in parentheses, $(24 - 2)$, is evaluated first, and the result, 22, is then divided by 7.

IDE detected
syntax error
caused by
missing
parenthesis

> ⚠ There is a syntax error on line 10. Code hinting may not work until you fix this error.

```
1   <!DOCTYPE HTML>
2   <html>
3       <head>
4           <title>Nesting Parentheses</title>
5       </head>
6
7       <body>
8           <script type="text/javascript">
9               var myValue1 = ((22 / 7) + 10) -3;
10              var myValue2 = 13 + (9 - 2 / (4 + 6);
11          </script>
12      </body>
13  </html>
14
```

This opening parenthesis is not
matched by a closing parthenthesis

Above: This example's second expression results in a syntax error.

Hot Tip

When nesting parentheses, always make sure that each opening parenthesis (is matched by a closing parenthesis). A syntax error occurs if there is a mismatch.

Nesting Parentheses

You will often find yourself needing to nest parentheses within parentheses, for example $((24 - 2) + 10) / 7$. In this scenario, it is the deepest nested expression that is evaluated first, followed by the next deepest nested, and so on.

STATEMENTS

At the top level of JavaScript's anatomy, we find the statement. All JavaScript instructions are contained within statements.

WHAT IS A STATEMENT?

A JavaScript statement encapsulates one or more expressions, and can be thought of as a discrete step or instruction within a script. Each statement in a script is executed in its entirety before the next statement is processed.

Making a Statement

Consider the following simple expression: `playerScore = 0;`. While this is an expression, it is also a statement, as indicated by the terminating semicolon `;`. A statement need not be any more complex than this, but they often are.

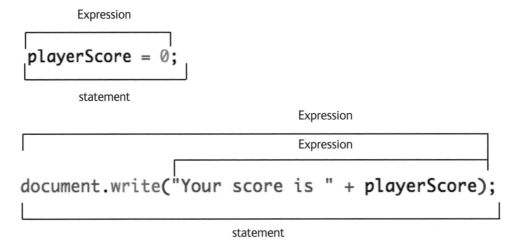

Above: Statements comprise one or more expressions.

Compound Expressions

We often build up quite complicated stacks of expressions within a statement, for example:

```
document.getElementsByTagName("body")[0].appendChild(document.
createElement("p")).innerHTML = "Hello World!";
```

This statement illustrates how expressions can be combined. It uses DOM programming techniques, introduced on page 109, to achieve the same outcome as the first script we wrote.

Above: Statements are often built out of compound expressions.

Hot Tip

Complex statements like the one on this page are usually much easier to write than to read. In fact, once you've got the hang of JavaScript, you'll probably find writing them to be curiously satisfying – even artistic.

Balancing Complexity Against Legibility

It's important to understand that lengthy and convoluted statements, such as the one above, can quite easily be broken down into a series of shorter, simpler statements.

All we do is distribute the expressions among more statements. However, in order to share the results of the expressions in one statement with the operators in another, we would need to store the result of each statement in a variable, so that the other statements have access to those values.

Balancing Speed Against Legibility

Creating and managing variables adds to the interpreter's workload, so complex statements comprising multiple expressions are generally executed more quickly than the same expressions broken down into multiple statements. So while choosing how simple – or complex – to make your statements is largely down to personal preference, you do need to think about how performance-critical the application is.

```
8    <script type="text/javascript">
9        //This compound statement...
10       document.getElementsByTagName("body")[0].appendChild(document.createElement("p")).inn
11       //...does the same as the following set of statements
12       var bodyElementsArray = document.getElementsByTagName("body");
13       var bodyElement = bodyElementsArray[0]; //Remember, there is only one body element
14       var newPara = document.createElement("p");
15       newPara.innerHTML = "Hello World!";
16       bodyElement.appendChild(newPara);
17
18   </script>
```

Above: Complex statements can be broken down into separate statements – or not.

```
● ○ ○                    Untitled — Edited
1: Decide how many cups of tea to make - call this number C
2: Lift kettle off base
3: Fill the kettle with enough water for C cups of tea
4: Add an extra half cup of water to allow for water lost as vapour
5: Place kettle back on base
6: Switch on kettle
7: Open cupboard that contains cups
8: Take C cups from cupboard
9: Place cups on bench near kettle
10: Shut cupboard
11: Open tea container
12: Take C tea bags from container and place one in each cup
13: Open fridge
14: Take milk from fridge and place on bench near kettle
15: Close fridge
16: Wait until kettle boils
```

Above: The perfect cuppa!

STATEMENT BLOCKS

Related statements can be grouped together into a block. This is done by wrapping the statements in braces – i.e. curly brackets: { and }. For example:

```
{
   var playerScore = 0;
   var playerName = 'Sarah';
   var playerAge = 29;
}
```

This technique has its uses, but doesn't achieve an awful lot. However, as we are about to discover, statement blocks become increasingly important the deeper we delve into JavaScript.

Hot Tip

Thinking about how to break down common tasks – such as making a cup of tea – into a series of concise, unambiguous instructions is a great way to practise the art of structuring JavaScript expressions and statements.

CONDITIONAL STATEMENTS

We often need to execute different statements based upon conditions that do not exist until a page has been loaded into a browser, and a user is interacting with it. This is when we reach for conditional statements.

IF STATEMENTS

With if, we test for the existence of a condition and then execute expressions should that condition exist. Its basic form looks like this:

```
if(condition) expressions;
```

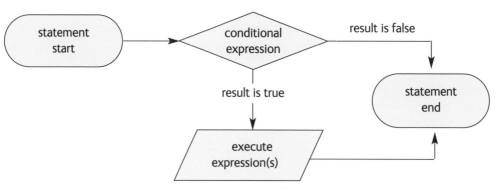

Above: Flowchart of a simple if statement.

USING IF STATEMENTS

When the interpreter encounters an if statement, it evaluates the expression contained inside the parentheses. In the event that the expression evaluates to true, the statement following the if is executed.

How an If Statement Works

Let's see how an if statement works using a simple example:

1. Create a new HTML document and enter the standard structural elements. Save the page as ifExample.html.

2. Create a new `<script>` element as a child of (i.e. inside) the `<head>` element. We're declaring it in the `<head>` to ensure it's available before the `<body>` element is rendered.

3. Add a simple variable declaration into this `<script>` element: var userAge = 36;. Although we've manually assigned a value to this variable, imagine that the user had actually provided this information. See the illustration, right.

4. Add another `<script>` element, this time as the child of the `<body>` element. Copy into this new `<script>` element the code shown in the illustration below.

5. Save your work and then open ifExample.html in Firefox.

```
1  <!DOCTYPE HTML>
2  <html>
3      <head>
4          <title>If Example</title>
5
6          <script type="text/javascript">
7              var userAge = 36;
8          </script>
9
10     </head>
```

Above: Step 3: Here you add a simple variable declaration.

```
12     <body>
13         <script type="text/javascript">
14             if(userAge > 16) alert("This is a kids zone - not for grown ups.");
15         </script>
16
17     </body>
```

Above: Step 4: Use this code as described in the text above.

Above: The if conditional expression evaluates to true, so we see the alert message.

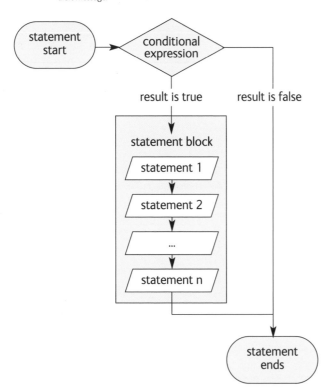

Above: Adding a statement block to an if statement.

How It Works

The condition expression of the if statement compares the userAge value against a literal value, 16. Because userAge evaluates to 36, and 36 is greater than 16, the if condition evaluates to true and the subsequent expression is evaluated.

Executing Multiple Statements

The above form of if can only execute a single statement when its condition is true, but we often need to execute multiple statements. To do this, we add a statement block following the condition expression (see Statement Blocks, page 63). The general form looks like this:

```
if(condition) {
    statement_1;
    statement_2;
    . . .
    statement_n;
}
```

Now, in the event that the condition evaluates to true, all of the statements within the statement block (the body of the if statement) are executed.

The Else Clause

The basic `if` statement can be expanded on via the addition of an `else` clause (we refer to it as a clause because it's a subsection of a larger `if` statement, and means nothing outside of an `if` statement). The general form is this:

```
if(condition) {
    statement(s);
} else {
    statement(s);
}
```

The statement block following `else` executes when the `if` statement's condition evaluates to `false`. Why not try adding an else clause to the last coding exercise (page 65)?

Hot Tip

The opening brace of a statement block can be directly following the closing parenthesis of the condition expression, or on its own line, or even just before the first statement. It's up to you.

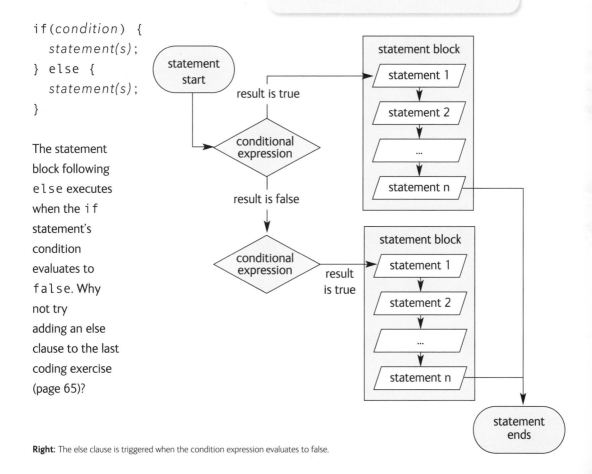

Right: The else clause is triggered when the condition expression evaluates to false.

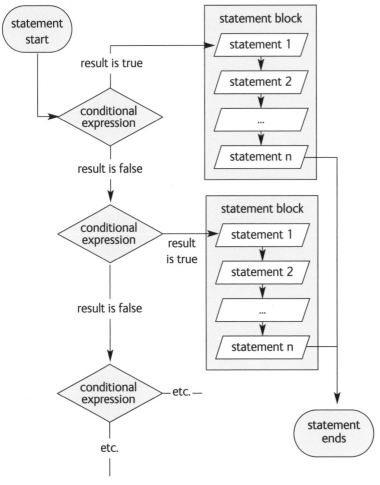

The Else If Clause

We can introduce a new conditional test in the event that the previous test evaluates to `false`. The general form looks like this:

```
if(condition)
{
    statement(s);
} else if(condition) {
    statement(s);
}
```

We can add as many `else if` clauses as we like, and also conclude with a final `else` clause that executes only when all preceding conditions evaluate to `false`.

Above: The `else if` clause adds more conditional tests to an `if` statement.

NESTING IF STATEMENTS

The `else if` clause creates a branching logical structure that is very common in programming. But beware: such structures become increasingly complex with each additional branch – we can often avoid them altogether by employing a different conditional statement.

THE SWITCH STATEMENT

Using switch is similar to if but rather than testing a condition for true or false, a switch statement selects a block of code to execute based on the result of the condition expression. The values to test for are specified in case sections. The general form is:

```
switch(condition) {
   case label_1:
      statement(s);
      break;
   case label_2:
      statement(s);
      break;
   ...
   default:
      statement(s);
      break;
}
```

How a Switch Statement Works

When the interpreter encounters a switch statement, it evaluates the condition expression and then looks in the statement block for a case **label** that matches the condition's result. If a match is found, all following statements are executed, including those contained in subsequent case sections.

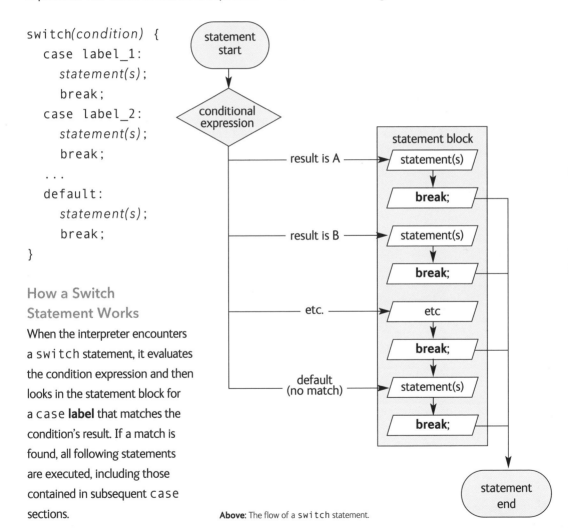

Above: The flow of a switch statement.

Breaking from a Case Section

In order to prevent subsequent case sections from being executed, we include a break keyword at the end of each case. This tells the interpreter to cease processing the statement block and resume execution at the first statement following the block.

Hot Tip

If you find that a structure of if-else-if statements is becoming too cumbersome to manage, a switch statement may be a more suitable approach.

Default Case

A switch statement can contain a special default section that is always triggered if encountered. This is typically placed at the end of the switch so that it is selected only if no case labels match the condition expression.case labels match the condition expression.

```
8    <script type="text/javascript">
9        //Imagine that an object named mediaObject exists on the page.
10       //mediaObject could refer to a video file or to an audio file,
11       //but when writing the code we don't know which it will be.
12       switch(mediaObject.mediaType) {
13           case "video":
14               alert("You are about to access a video");
15               //statements that cause the video to load and play
16               break;
17           case "audio":
18               alert("You are about to access an audio recording");
19               //statements that cause the audio to load and play
20               break;
21           default:
22               alert("Cannot determine the media type");
23       }
24
25   </script>
```

Above: This imaginary script shows how a switch statement can be used.

LOOP STATEMENTS

We often need to run the same set of statements against a collection of different values, or repeat statements a certain number of times – this is where loops come in.

WHILE LOOPS

The simplest form of loop statement is known as the `while` loop. Its general form is:

```
while(condition) {
   statement(s);
}
```

Hot Tip

Caution: if you code loops incorrectly, you may trigger an infinite loop, where the interpreter gets stuck processing the same loop statement indefinitely.

If the condition evaluates to `true`, the statement(s) contained in the code block following the condition are executed, then the condition is tested again. If still true, the process is repeated. This continues until the condition evaluates to `false`.

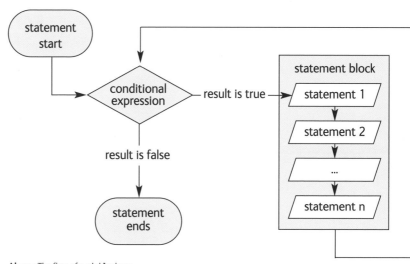

Above: The flow of a `while` loop.

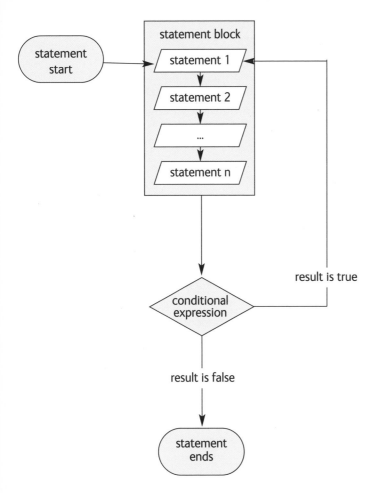

Above: The flow of a do while loop.

DO WHILE LOOPS

These loops are very similar to while loops, except the condition is evaluated only after the statement block has been executed. If the condition resolves to true, the statement block is repeated and the condition evaluated once more. Here's how it looks:

```
do {
    statement(s);
} while(condition);
```

FOR LOOPS

The for loop is often used for processing the elements of an array, because it simplifies executing the same statement block against each element in the array. The for loop's declaration can appear a little daunting – let's take a look at it before analysing what it means:

```
for(initialize ; condition ; iteration ) {
    statement(s);
}
```

Elements of a For Loop

The three elements of a for loop are expressions that control the reiteration of the loop:

- **initialize:** This expression is evaluated once and creates an initial index for the loop; the index is just a number, typically used to count the number of loop iterations that have occurred.

- **condition:** This is the expression that is tested to see whether the loop repeats or not. In most circumstances, the condition expression tests the value of the index against some other value, such as an array's length.

- **iteration:** This expression is evaluated after the loop's statement block has been executed, and its intended use is to modify the value of the index before the next iteration.

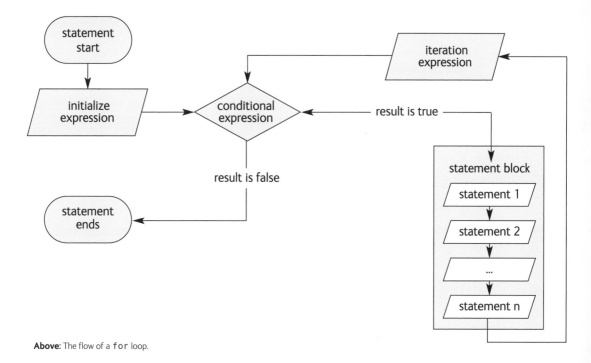

Above: The flow of a for loop.

Using a For Loop

In the exercise on page 41, we created two objects that represented questions in a quiz – we're going to build on that idea.

1. Create a new folder and call it SimpleQuiz. Create a subfolder and call it js – this is where we'll be storing external script files in later examples.

2. Create a new HTML document containing the common structural elements, and save it in the new folder as simpleQuiz.html. Also create a new JavaScript document and save it in the js subfolder as quizQuestions.js.

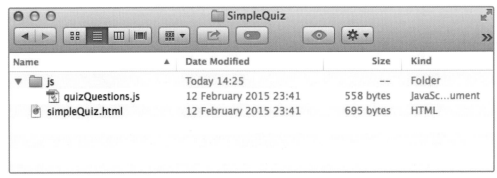

Above: Create an outer folder and scripts subfolder for a quiz application, and save the files within it.

3. Return to the HTML document. Add a `<script>` element as a child of the `<head>` element, setting

```
1  <!DOCTYPE HTML>
2  <html>
3      <head>
4          <title>A Simple Quiz</title>
5
6          <script type="text/javascript" src="js/quizQuestions.js"></script>
7      </head>
8
9      <body>
10     </body>
11 </html>
12
```

Above: Step 3: Add the code shown here into your HTML document.

its `type` attribute to `"text/javascript"` and its `src` attribute to `"js/quizQuestions.js"`. See the illustration below.

4. Go to quizQuestions.js, where we're going to define the questions themselves. At the top of the file, declare an array variable named `questions`.

5. Now we'll add a question by declaring object and array literals within the `push()` method's parentheses, as shown in the illustration below. You can copy our questions and answers, or come up with your own.

> # Hot Tip
>
> **We're no longer going to remind you to add the type attribute to a `<script>` element – take it as read that you should.**

```
1  var questions = [];
2
3  //QUESTION 1
4  questions.push({
5      questionText: "Approximately how far away from the Earth is the Sun?",
6      answers: ["200 miles", "93,000,000 miles", "49,000,000 miles", "150,000 miles"],
7      correctAnswerIndex: 1}
8  );
9
10 //QUESTION 2
11 questions.push({
12     questionText: "How many planets are there in our solar system?",
13     answers: ["6", "7", "8", "9"],
14     correctAnswerIndex: 2}
15 );
16
17 //QUESTION 3
18 questions.push({
19     questionText: "Which of these is a moon of Jupiter?",
20     answers: ["Ganymede", "Miranda", "Enceladus", "Mars"],
21     correctAnswerIndex: 0}
22 );
23
```

Above: Step 5: Why not create your own questions and answers?

6. Save the JavaScript document, then in your editor, return to the HTML document.

```
11      <script type="text/javascript">
12          for(var i = 0; i < questions.length ; i++) {
13              document.write("<h2>QUESTION" + (i + 1) + "</h2>");
14              document.write("<p>" + questions[i].questionText + "</p>");
15              document.write("<p>A1: " + questions[i].answers[0] + "</p>");
16              document.write("<p>A2: " + questions[i].answers[1] + "</p>");
17              document.write("<p>A3: " + questions[i].answers[2] + "</p>");
18              document.write("<p>A4: " + questions[i].answers[3] + "</p>");
19          }
20      </script>
21
```

Above: Step 7: Add the code shown here into your HTML document.

7. Add a new `<script>` element as a child of the `<body>` element – add the code shown in the illustration above.

9. Save your work and launch the HTML page in Firefox.

How It Works

The first `<script>` element is easy enough – it links to a script in which we declare objects that represent the questions in our quiz, and stores these in an array called `questions`. This array is accessible to all scripts in the page, and is defined in the `<head>` so that we can be sure it's available when processing the page's `<body>`.

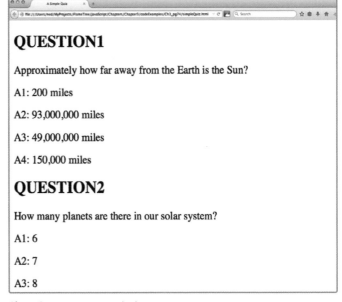

QUESTION1

Approximately how far away from the Earth is the Sun?

A1: 200 miles

A2: 93,000,000 miles

A3: 49,000,000 miles

A4: 150,000 miles

QUESTION2

How many planets are there in our solar system?

A1: 6

A2: 7

A3: 8

Above: Our quiz is starting to take shape.

Now let's look at the `for` loop in the second `<script>` element. The index is initialized to 0. Then the condition `i < questions.length` is evaluated. When `i` is 0 the condition evaluates to `true`, so the loop body is executed, and text is written to the page using the familiar `document.write()` technique. The important thing to note is that we use the loop index, `i`, to access each element of the `questions` array in turn.

Once the statement block has completed, the iteration expression, `i++`, is evaluated, adding 1 to the index, and the condition is tested once more. The process repeats until the condition evaluates to `false`.

EXITING FROM A LOOP OR ITERATION

We can exit a loop at any time by writing the `break` keyword, causing script execution to resume at the first statement following the loop. We can also exit from the current iteration of a loop using `continue`, which instructs the interpreter to evaluate the iteration and condition expressions immediately, and then continue looping if required.

```
10      <body>
11          <script type="text/javascript">
12              for(var i = 0; i < questions.length ; i++) {
13                  if(typeof i != "Number") {
14                      //if i is not a number it can't be an index - something's
15                      //gone wrong so exit the loop
16                      break;
17                  } else if(questions[i].questionText = "") {
18                      //if the question has no question text then skip this
19                      //iteration
20                      continue;
21                  } else {
22                      //all's fine - render the question
23                      document.write("<h2>QUESTION" + (i + 1) + "</h2>");
24                      document.write("<p>" + questions[i].questionText + "</p>");
25                      document.write("<p>A1: " + questions[i].answers[0] + "</p>");
26                      document.write("<p>A2: " + questions[i].answers[1] + "</p>");
27                      document.write("<p>A3: " + questions[i].answers[2] + "</p>");
28                      document.write("<p>A4: " + questions[i].answers[3] + "</p>");
29                  }
30              }
31          </script>
32
33      </body>
34  </html>
```

Above: The `continue` and `break` statements enable us respectively to skip an iteration or exit a loop entirely.

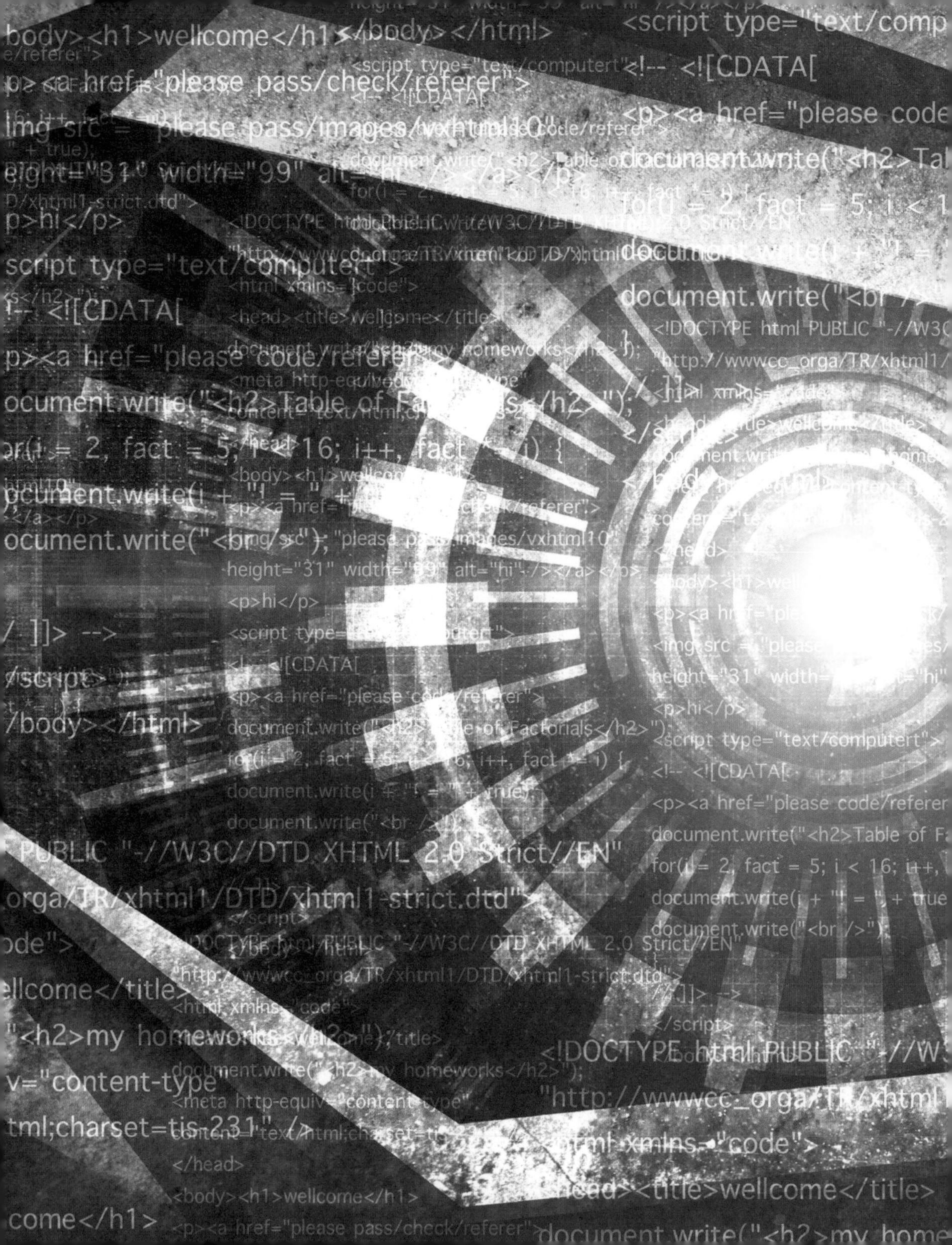

body><h1>wellcome</h1></body></html>   <script type="text/comp

p><a href="please pass/check/referer">

img src ="please pass/images/vxhtml10" code/referer>

eight="31" width="99" alt=   document.write("<h2>Table of   document.write("<h2>Tal

p>hi</p>   for(i = 2, fact = 5; i < 1

script type="text/computert">   document.write() + "! =

!-- <![CDATA[document.write("

p><a href="please code/referer">

ocument.write("<h2>Table of Factorials</h2>");

br(i = 2, fact = 5; i < 16; i++, fact *= i) {

ocument.write(i + "! =" + true);

ocument.write("<img src"; "please pass/images/vxhtml10"

height="31" width="99" alt="hi"/></a></p>

<p>hi</p>

/]]> -->   <script type=

/script>

/body></html>   document.write("<h2>Table of Factorials</h2>")

          for(i = 2, fact = 5; i < 16; i++, fact *= i) {

          document.write(i + "! =" + true)

          document.write("<br />")

PUBLIC "-//W3C//DTD XHTML 2.0 Strict//EN"

orga/TR/xhtml1/DTD/xhtml1-strict.dtd">

ode">

llcome</title>

"<h2>my homeworks</h2>");

v="content-type

tml;charset=tis-231" />

come</h1>   <p><a href="please pass/check/referer">

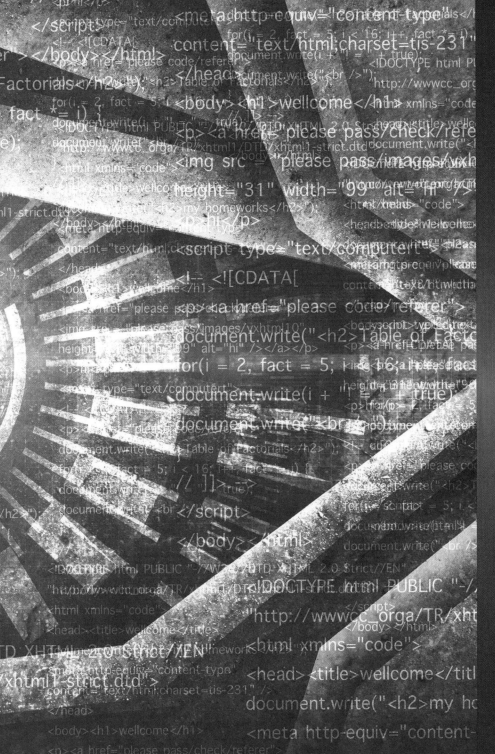

FUNCTIONS & CLASSES OF JAVASCRIPT

FUNCTIONS IN JAVASCRIPT

A function is a collection of statements that can be executed by referring to an identifier assigned to the function. They are key to creating reusable blocks of code that can be called on when needed.

BUILT-IN FUNCTIONS

JavaScript has a number of functions built into the language – in fact, we've already been using one: the `alert()` function. When we use a function's name in a script, we are **calling** or **invoking** the function – this is signified by the parentheses that follow the function name. Using these parentheses, we can also pass data – referred to as **arguments** – to the function.

Function Arguments

Arguments are values that are passed to a function, and which the functions can use. For example, with the alert() function call, we place the message string that we want the dialogue box to display within the parentheses. Some functions need to be passed to more than one argument – in this case, we separate each argument with a comma.

NAMED FUNCTIONS

There are a couple of techniques for creating functions, but the first is easy – we use the function keyword. It looks like this:

```
function functionName(parameter_1, parameter_2, ... ,
parameter_n) {
   statement(s);
}
```

```
2  function showMessageToUser(userName, message) {
3      alert("Hi " + userName + ", " + message);
4  }
5
6  showMessageToUser("Oliver", "Your function is working");
7
```

Above: A simple function definition and a call to that function.

functionName is the name given to the function – it must follow the rules for identifier naming (*see* page 149). The function definition can include a comma-separated list of **parameters** – these these are identifiers that receive the values passed as arguments in the call to the function, and can be used by the statements within the function. A statement block follows the parentheses – this is known as the body of the function, and is executed whenever the function is invoked.

Hot Tip

When passing arguments in a function call, they must be listed in the same order as the parameters are listed in the function definition.

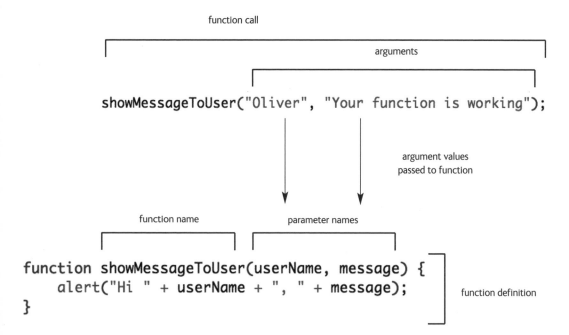

Above: Function calls assign values to the parameters named in the function definition.

Creating a Named Function

In the previous exercise, we wrote some code that rendered the content of a custom question object on the page – let's wrap that in a reusable function.

1. In your editor, create a new JavaScript file and save it as quizFunctions.js within the js subfolder of our SimpleQuiz folder.

2. Add the function declaration, as shown in the illustration, right. Notice that we've named a single parameter, *questionIndex* – the idea is that we will pass an index value as an argument when we invoke the function.

```
1
2  function renderQuestionAtIndex(questionIndex) {
3      //function statements will go here...
4  }
```

Above: Step 2: Add this function declaration into your JavaScript file.

3. Open simpleQuiz.html in your editor. Add a new `<script>` element as a child of the `<head>` element, and set its `src` attribute to `"js/quizFunctions.js"`.

4. Locate the `for` loop in the HTML document, then delete all of the statements from the body of the loop and replace them with a call to our new function,

```
6          <script type="text/javascript" src="js/quizQuestions.js"></script>
7          <script type="text/javascript" src="js/quizFunctions.js"></script>
8
9      </head>
10
11     <body>
12         <script type="text/javascript">
13             for(var i = 0; i < questions.length ; i++) {
14                 renderQuestionAtIndex(i);
15             }
16         </script>
17
18     </body>
```

Above: Step 4: Delete the statements and replace them as described in the text above.

`renderQuestionAtIndex(i);`, as in the illustration on the previous page. Note that we're passing the loop index value to the function, which will use it to access an element of the `questions` array.

5. Save the HTML document and return to quizFunctions.js. Add the code shown in the illustration below to the body of the `renderQuestionAtIndex()` function.

```
1
2  function renderQuestionAtIndex(questionIndex) {
3      document.write("<h2>QUESTION " + (questionIndex + 1) + "</h2>");
4      var questionObject = questions[questionIndex];
5      document.write("<p>" + questionObject.question + "</p>");
6      document.write("<p>A1: " + questionObject.answers[0] + "</p>");
7      document.write("<p>A2: " + questionObject.answers[1] + "</p>");
8      document.write("<p>A3: " + questionObject.answers[2] + "</p>");
9      document.write("<p>A4: " + questionObject.answers[3] + "</p>");
10 }
```

Above: Step 5: Add the code shown here to the function body.

6. Notice that the function body is almost identical to the code we just deleted, but now we can render a question just by passing an index value to the function.

7. Save your work and open the page in Firefox. All being well, you should see the exact same result as before.

RETURNING A VALUE FROM A FUNCTION

We often want to process the values we pass to a function in some way, and to return the result of that calculation to the calling expression – the returned value becomes the value of the function call. We do this with the `return` keyword.

Using the Return Keyword

When the interpreter encounters `return`, it ceases processing of the function and returns to the calling expression. If the function needs to send a value back to the calling expression, we place the value in parentheses following the `return` keyword – for example,

`return(functionResult);`.

Hot Tip

It's good practice to try to arrange things so that there's only one return keyword in a function – but this isn't always achievable.

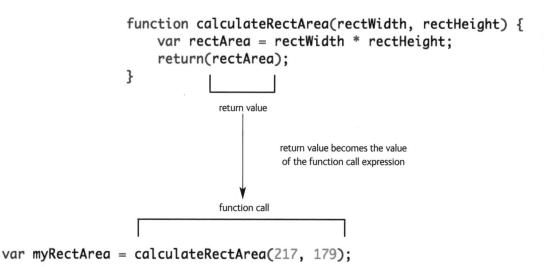

```
function calculateRectArea(rectWidth, rectHeight) {
    var rectArea = rectWidth * rectHeight;
    return(rectArea);
}
```

return value

return value becomes the value
of the function call expression

function call

```
var myRectArea = calculateRectArea(217, 179);
```

Above: The value returned by a function becomes the value of the function call expression.

Using Return When Checking a Quiz Answer

Our quiz needs to be able to determine whether the user has selected a correct answer – let's write a function for that now.

1. Open quizFunctions.js in your editor, and add a new function called checkUserAnswer() – see the illustration below. The function will receive two arguments – a question index and an answer index – that allow the function to determine the question that's to be checked and the answer that was given.

```
11  function checkUserAnswer(questionIndex, answerIndex) {
12        //function statements will go here...
13  }
14
```

Above: Step 1: Add a new function as shown here.

2. Enter the code shown in the illustration below and then save your work.

```
10
11  function checkUserAnswer(questionIndex, answerIndex) {
12      var questionObject = questions[questionIndex];
13      var theResult;
14      if(questionObject.correctAnswerIndex == answerIndex) {
15          theResult = true;
16      } else {
17          theResult = false;
18      }
19      return(theResult);
20  }
21
```

Above: Step 2: Enter the code shown here.

3. Nothing new happens if you launch the page, because we aren't triggering the new function in any way – we'll get to that when we look at Events on page 240.

ANONYMOUS FUNCTIONS

In JavaScript, a function is just another form of data. This means that you can create a function and assign it to a variable or object property. Such functions are called anonymous functions, because they don't have a function name.

Declaring an Anonymous Function

We declare an anonymous function by assigning a function literal to a variable or object property. The general form looks like this:

```
var myAnonymousFunction = function(parameter(s)) {
    statement(s);
}
```

Invoking an Anonymous Function

Invoking an anonymous function is no different to invoking a named one; we just use a variable name or property reference instead of a function name. To all intents and purposes, this is identical to invoking a named function.

```
1  //This is a named function...
2  function calculateRectArea(rectWidth, rectHeight) {
3      return(rectWidth * rectHeight);
4  }
5
6  //This is an anonymous function...
7  var calculateRectHypotenuse = function(rectWidth, rectHeight) {
8      var widthSquared = rectWidth * rectWidth;
9      var heightSquared = rectHeight * rectHeight;
10     return(Math.sqrt(widthSquared + heightSquared)); //Math.sqrt() calculates a square root
11 }
12
13 //Calls to either function have the same general form:
14 var myRectArea = calculateRectArea(49, 28);
15 var myRectHypotenuse = calculateRectHypotenuse(49, 28);
16
```

Above: Named and anonymous functions are called in the same way.

VARIABLE SCOPE

When a variable is declared outside of any functions or statement blocks, it is available from anywhere in the web page, so is known as a **global** variable. Another way of putting this is that the variable exists within the global **scope**. Conversely, variables declared within a function are only accessible from within that function – they are said to be within the function's scope.

The Scope Chain

Scope is hierarchical – one scope is nested within another. For example, named functions always exist in the global scope. An expression can only access variables that are in the same scope as – or are further up the scope chain than – the expression.

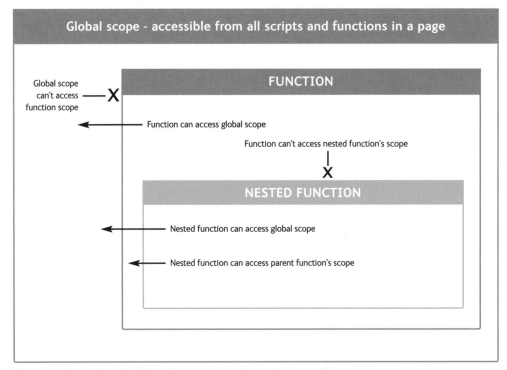

Above: Variable scope is hierarchical. A variable in one scope can't access deeper-nested scopes.

NAMESPACES

We create a lot of named objects – variables and functions – in JavaScript, and the name of each should be unique within its own scope. If it isn't unique, a name clash occurs, and things go badly wrong.

WHAT IS A NAMESPACE?

Namespaces are notional spaces or contexts in which a set of unique names can be defined. Put another way, two names can be identical so long as they exist in different namespaces. Namespaces are important because without them, we run the risk of encountering name clashes.

Hot Tip

The concept of namespaces can seem confusing initially, but is actually quite simple in practice – we all use them all the time.

NOUN
Dog: A four-legged domesticated animal often kept as a pet

VERB
Dog: To persistently pursue or pester

NOUN
Shoot: A young branch stemming from the main branch of a tree or plant

VERB
Shoot: The act of firing a gun or cannon

NOUN
Dope: A stupid or indolent person

VERB
Dope: To administer drugs

Above: We can think of verbs and nouns as being examples of real-world namespaces – a name can appear in both, yet remain distinct.

What is a Name Clash?

A name clash occurs when a name given to an object in a page is used by another object within the same page. Any expression that uses this name may not get back the data it expects or requires, leading to hard-to-trace bugs and errors.

Pollution of the Global Namespace

The name of every named function and every global variable exists within the global namespace. With large projects, this namespace can become littered with many different names. Having third-party scripts in a page can make matters considerably worse. The more polluted the global namespace becomes, the more likely that you will encounter name clashes.

Above: The global namespace can become somewhat messy.

SIMULATING NAMESPACES IN JAVASCRIPT

Unlike some languages, JavaScript does not have formal notation for creating namespaces. However, remember that everything in JavaScript is an object – an upshot of this is that we can create an object in the global namespace and then define all of our variables and functions within this object. Our names don't pollute the global namespace, and if we choose the namespace object's name wisely, we won't end up using the same one as is used in other scripts.

Hot Tip

The name of a named function exists in the global namespace. In contrast, anonymous functions can be assigned to an object property, thereby removing their identifiers from the global namespace.

```
1
2  var myNamespace = {};
3
4  myNamespace.calculateRectArea = function(rectWidth, rectHeight) {
5      return(rectWidth * rectHeight);
6  }
7
```

Above: Anonymous functions can be assigned to object properties so that they don't pollute the global namespace.

Choosing a Name for a Namespace

Given that a namespace's name has to exist in the global namespace, it is entirely possible to get a name clash with another namespace's name. The trick to avoiding this is to choose a name

that nobody else is likely to be using. How do you do this? Easy – base the namespace name on your website's domain name. Typically, we reverse the name, so if your domain name is mydomain.com, your namespace would be `com.mydomain`. You could then extend this further with a per-application and/or per-module name – for example, `com.mydomain.myApplication`.

Global scope namespace

Global identifiers and named functions

com

com.mydomain

identifiers that refer to the functions and values used by your scripts

com.otherdomain

identifiers that refer to the functions and values defined by 3rd party scripts that are attached to your page. The have their own namespace so won't crash with your names.

Above: JavaScript simulates namespaces using objects. Reversing your domain name is the best way to ensure your names don't clash with others'.

Creating a Namespace

Let's create a namespace for the objects in our Simple Quiz project.

1. Open quizQuestions.js in your editor and create a couple of empty lines at the top of the document.

2. We're going to use com.flametreepublishing as our namespace – this means we need to create an object called com inside the global namespace and another called flametreepublishing inside the com object.

```
1  var com;
2  if(!com) {
3      com = {};
4  }
5  if(!com.flametreepublishing) {
6      com.flametreepublishing = {};
7  }
```

Above: Step 3: Copy the code shown here into your editor.

3. Copy the code shown in the illustration (right). After declaring – but not initializing – com, we test that each namespace object does not exist before initializing it (see Logical NOT Operator, page 57). This is to avoid initializing an existing namespace.

```
9   com.flametreepublishing.questions = [];
10
11  //QUESTION 1
12  com.flametreepublishing.questions.push({
13      question: "Approximately how far away from the Earth is the Sun?",
14      answers: ["200 miles", "93,000,000 miles", "49,000,000 miles", "150,000 miles"],
15      correctAnswerIndex: 1}
16  );
17
18  //QUESTION 2
19  com.flametreepublishing.questions.push({
20      question: "How many planets are there in our solar system?",
21      answers: ["6", "7", "8", "9"],
22      correctAnswerIndex: 2}
23  );
24
25  //QUESTION 3
26  com.flametreepublishing.questions.push({
27      question: "Which of these is a moon of Jupiter?",
28      answers: ["Ganymede", "Miranda", "Enceladus", "Mars"],
```

4. Now we'll adapt the rest of the script so that it uses the new namespace – see the un-dimmed sections of the illustration, right.

Above: Step 4: Adapt the script as highlighted here.

5. Save quizQuestions.js and open quizFunctions.js. It is good practice to include your namespace declaration at the top of all scripts, so copy it to the top of quizFunctions.js.

```
 9  com.flametreepublishing.renderQuestionAtIndex = function(questionIndex) {
10      document.write("<h2>QUESTION " + (questionIndex + 1) + "</h2>");
11      var questionObject = com.flametreepublishing.questions[questionIndex];
12      document.write("<p>" + questionObject.question + "</p>");
13      document.write("<p>A1:  " + questionObject.answers[0] + "</p>");
14      document.write("<p>A2:  " + questionObject.answers[1] + "</p>");
15      document.write("<p>A3:  " + questionObject.answers[2] + "</p>");
16      document.write("<p>A4:  " + questionObject.answers[3] + "</p>");
17  }
18
19  com.flametreepublishing.checkUserAnswer = function(questionIndex, answerIndex) {
20      var questionObject = com.flametreepublishing.questions[questionIndex];
21      var theResult;
```

Above: Step 6: Update the references as highlighted here.

6. In order to place the functions within our namespace, we need to change them to anonymous functions. We also need to update all references to the `questions` array – see the highlighted portions of the illustration above.

7. Save the document and then open simpleQuiz.html in your editor. Locate the `for` loop and update its condition expression and function call, as shown in the illustration below.

```
12          <script type="text/javascript">
13              for(var i = 0; i < com.flametreepublishing.questions.length ; i++) {
14                  com.flametreepublishing.renderQuestionAtIndex(i);
15              }
16          </script>
```

Above: Step 7: Update the condition expression and function call as shown here.

8. Save your work and open the page in Firefox – again, it should look identical to previously, but underneath we have a pristine and unpolluted namespace.

OBJECT ORIENTED PROGRAMMING

Object oriented programming – OOP – is an approach to programming that places objects at the heart of everything. While JavaScript is not a true OOP language, because it lacks specific constructs that are requirements for true OOP, it can be – and normally is – used in an OOP style.

WHY USE OOP TECHNIQUES?

Far too many words have been written by others about the relative merits and drawbacks of OOP compared to other approaches to programming – and we're not going to add to them. Suffice it to say that one of the most compelling features of OOP is that it organizes things in much the same way as our human brains do. For this reason if no other, it is the most widely used approach to programming.

Above: OOP structures code in much the same way as humans structure thoughts.

HOW WE CLASSIFY THINGS

When we think about a thing in the physical world, that thing is normally part of a family of similar things; this family is in turn part of a larger grouping, and so on. These groupings classify the thing we were thinking about in the first place.

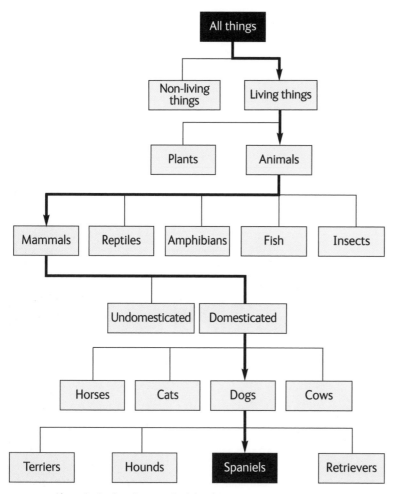

Above: By classifying things, we also define them.

For example, we could classify a spaniel as a dog, as domesticated, as a mammal, as an animal, and as a living thing. This gives a chain of classification that defines something dog-like. Each point in that chain specifies characteristics that hone the definition – the number of legs an animal has, for instance, or the smoothness of a dog's fur.

With sufficient classification and definition of characteristics, we can determine that something is a spaniel as opposed to anything else in the entire universe; we do this without even thinking about it.

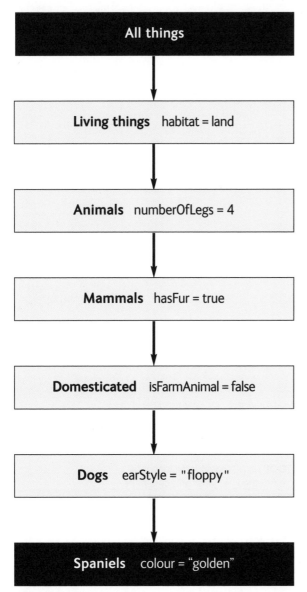

All things

Living things   habitat = land

Animals   numberOfLegs = 4

Mammals   hasFur = true

Domesticated   isFarmAnimal = false

Dogs   earStyle = "floppy"

Spaniels   colour = "golden"

Above: In the physical world, characteristics are inherited and become an intrinsic part of a thing's definition – the same is true in OOP.

CLASSES IN OOP

OOP harnesses exactly this system of hierarchical classification. We write scripts called **classes** that define **properties**. The properties describe the characteristics of – and are intrinsic to – the class. Classes also define **methods**, these being functions that operate on objects of the class.

A class inherits the properties and methods of its ancestor classes, taking on aspects of their characteristics and behaviour. This is much like a spaniel's inherent spaniel-ness being a function of the compounded characteristics and classifications it belongs to.

Constructors and Instances

The code you write in a class script is like a template – it describes the properties and methods that define objects of that class.

However, this class definition is not an object of that class – to create one of those, we must call the class's **constructor** function, because it is this that generates an object from the class definition. This generated object is known as an **instance** of the class, so the act of calling the class constructor is often referred to as **instantiating** the class.

A Massive Topic

OOP is a very deep subject that we aren't going to delve into – if it's something you want to explore, Google 'OOP' and take your pick from the thousands of results.
What we are going to do, though, is find out how to create and use basic custom classes in JavaScript.

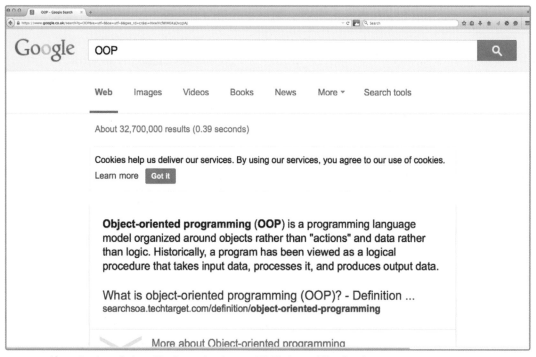

Above: Google can find over 33 million articles relating to OOP. That's an awful lot of reading.

JAVASCRIPT CLASSES

We've already been working with JavaScript classes – number, string and array are all built-in classes. They all inherit some of their characteristics from the object class – in OOP parlance, this makes the object the **superclass** of those other classes.

We've also been working with class methods; for example, `write` is a method of the HTMLDocument class – we've used it as `document.write()`. (`document` is an instance of the HTMLDocument class.) These classes are built into the language, but we can also build our own.

Defining a Custom Class

The questions in our Simple Quiz application are currently defined in generic objects – let's develop a QuizQuestion class instead.

1. Create a new JavaScript document and save it in your Simple Quiz's js folder as QuizQuestion.js. Also create a `<script>` element in the `<head>` of simpleQuiz.html and link it to this new script. See the illustration below.

```
1  <!DOCTYPE HTML>
2  <html>
3      <head>
4          <title>A Simple Quiz</title>
5
6          <script type="text/javascript" src="js/QuizQuestion.js"></script>
7          <script type="text/javascript" src="js/quizQuestions.js"></script>
8          <script type="text/javascript" src="js/quizFunctions.js"></script>
9
10     </head>
11
12     <body>
13         <script type="text/javascript">
14             for(var i = 0; i < com.flametreepublishing.questions.length ; i++)
15                 com.flametreepublishing.renderQuestionAtIndex(i);
```

Above: Step 1: Create a new JavaScript document as shown here.

2. Add our namespace declaration at the top of QuizQuestion.js (*see* page 217).

3. We're going to call this class QuizQuestion, so the first thing to do is define the constructor function – see the illustration below. The constructor function has the same name as the class.

```
1  var com;
2  if(!com) {
3      com = {};
4  }
5  if(!com.flametreepublishing) {
6      com.flametreepublishing = {};
7  }
8
9  com.flametreepublishing.QuizQuestion = function(aQuestionNum, aQuestionText, aAnswers, aCorrectAnswerIndex) {
10
11 }
```

Above: Step 3: Define the constructor function as shown here.

4. As you see, the constructor expects four parameters. These correspond to the properties we want QuizQuestion instances to have; we've added a leading 'a' to the names so they are distinct from the similarly named class properties.

5. Add the code highlighted in the illustration above to the body of the constructor.

```
9   com.flametreepublishing.QuizQuestion = function(aQuestionNum,
10                                                   aQuestionText,
11                                                   aAnswers,
12                                                   aCorrectAnswerIndex) {
13      this.questionNum = aQuestionNum;
14      this.questionText = aQuestionText;
15      this.answers = aAnswers;
16      this.correctAnswerIndex = aCorrectAnswerIndex;
17  }
18
```

Above: Step 5: Add the code highlighted here.

Here, we meet the `this` keyword for the first time – see above.

6. Save your work.

CREATING AN INSTANCE

Now that the constructor is defined, we can create a QuizQuestion instance by using the `new` keyword, like this:

```
new com.flametreepublishing.QuizQuestion(arguments);
```

Recall that the QuizQuestion constructor function expects four arguments to be passed to it: the question number, the question text, the array of possible answers, and the index of the correct answer. These all need to be included within the parentheses following the constructor name when instantiating the class – we'll come back to this shortly.

> ## Hot Tip
>
> By convention, we name classes with a leading upper-case character, and instances with a leading lower-case character.

```
20    new com.flametreepublishing.QuizQuestion(
21        1,
22        "Approximately how far away from the Earth is the Sun?",
23        ["200 miles", "93,000,000 miles", "49,000,000 miles", "150,000 miles"],
24        1
25    )
26
```

Above: Instantiating a class creates an object of that class which we can then work with.

THE THIS KEYWORD

The last walkthrough introduced the special `this` keyword. When used in a constructor function, `this` refers to the instance that's under construction.

In the code we've just written, there are four statements starting with `this` – these assign the argument values sent to the constructor to the new instance. By assigning these values to `this`, we assign them to the new instance.

When `this` is used in a class method, it refers to the specific instance of the class that the method is being executed on. This will become clearer over the coming exercises.

CLASS METHODS

A method is similar to a function. In simple terms, where a function is a stand alone entity that can have objects passed to it, a method is part and parcel of an object, and operates from the context of that object.

We've already met a few methods of the built-in classes – for example, the `push()` method of the array class. When we call `push()`, we do so via an instance of the array class: `myArray.push(newValue)`, hence it is a method.

The Prototype Object

As has been mentioned previously, the JavaScript object class holds an exalted place within the language – it is the class upon which all other classes are based. The upshot is that all other classes, including our own custom classes, inherit the methods and properties of the object class. One such property is called `prototype` – this is where the methods of a class should be defined. Let's see how.

```
25
26  //QUESTION 1
27  com.flametreepublishing.questions.push({
28      question: "Approximately how far away from the Earth is the Sun?",
29      answers: ["200 miles", "93,000,000 miles", "49,000,000 miles", "150,000 miles"],
30      correctAnswerIndex: 1}
31  );
32
```

Above: We've already met the `push()` method of the array class (note that `com.flametreepublishing.questions` is an instance of the array class).

Defining Class Methods

We currently have a function in our quiz, `checkUserAnswer`, which would be better as a method of our new QuizQuestion class.

1. Open QuizQuestion.js in your editor.

```
15
16  com.flametreepublishing.QuizQuestion.prototype.checkUserAnswer = function(answerIndex) {
17      var theResult;
18      if(answerIndex == this.correctAnswerIndex) {
19          theResult = true;
20      } else {
21          theResult = false;
22      }
23      return(theResult);
24  }
```

Above: Step 2: Insert the method definition as shown here.

2. Create a couple of empty lines below the constructor and then type the `checkUserAnswer` method definition shown in the illustration on the previous page. This uses much the same logic as our earlier function of the same name.

3. Note that the method name has to be prefixed by the namespace, the class name, and the `prototype` property reference. This can become somewhat long-winded, but is unavoidable.

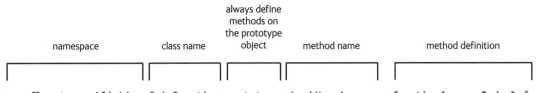

namespace   class name   always define methods on the prototype object   method name   method definition

```
com.flametreepublishing.QuizQuestion.prototype.checkUserAnswer = function(answerIndex) {
```

Above: Method names can become a bit long-winded, but they have a simple structure.

4. While we're here, let's make the question self-rendering. The code for this is shown in the illustration below and should be familiar by now.

5. Save your work.

```
26
27  com.flametreepublishing.QuizQuestion.prototype.renderQuestion = function() {
28      document.write("<h2>QUESTION " + this.questionNum + "</h2>");
29      document.write("<p>" + this.questionText + "</p>");
30      document.write("<p>A1: " + this.answers[0] + "</p>");
31      document.write("<p>A2: " + this.answers[1] + "</p>");
32      document.write("<p>A3: " + this.answers[2] + "</p>");
33      document.write("<p>A4: " + this.answers[3] + "</p>");
34  }
35
```

Above: Step 4: The code here will make the question self-rendering.

CREATING A MAIN CLASS

When building a JavaScript application, it is common to create a main or central class in which to define properties and methods that are global to the application. The idea is that we create a single instance of this class, and use this as the central kicking-off and reference point for everything else in the application.

A SimpleQuiz Class

Let's create a main class for our Simple Quiz application.

1. Create a new JavaScript document and save it in the project's js folder as SimpleQuiz.js.

2. Open simpleQuiz.html in your editor. Add a `<script>` element that links to the new SimpleQuiz.js script, and delete the `<script>` elements that link to quizQuestions.js and quizFunctions.js. Save the HTML file and switch back to SimpleQuiz.js. See the illustration, right.

```
1  <!DOCTYPE HTML>
2  <html>
3      <head>
4          <title>A Simple Quiz</title>
5
6          <script type="text/javascript" src="js/QuizQuestion.js"></script>
7          <script type="text/javascript" src="js/SimpleQuiz.js"></script>
8
9      </head>
```

Above: Step 2: Add the code as shown here.

3. Add our standard namespace declaration and create a constructor function – see the illustration, right.

```
1  var com;
2  if(!com) {
3      com = {};
4  }
5  if(!com.flametreepublishing) {
6      com.flametreepublishing = {};
7  }
8
9  com.flametreepublishing.SimpleQuiz = function() {
10
11 }
```

Above: Step 3: Create a constructor function as shown here.

4. We still need an array in which to store the QuizQuestion objects – we'll make this a property of the SimpleQuiz class by declaring and initializing it in the constructor as shown in the illustration, right.

```
8
9  com.flametreepublishing.SimpleQuiz = function() {
10     this.questions = [];
11 }
12
```

Above: Step 4: Declare and initialize the array as shown here.

```
 9  com.flametreepublishing.SimpleQuiz = function() {
10      this.questions = [];
11      this.loadQuestions();
12  }
13
14  com.flametreepublishing.SimpleQuiz.prototype.loadQuestions = function() {
15      //QUESTION 1
16      this.questions.push(
17          new com.flametreepublishing.QuizQuestion(
18              1,
19              "Approximately how far away from the Earth is the Sun?",
20              ["200 miles", "93,000,000 miles", "49,000,000 miles", "150,000 miles"],
21              1
22          )
23      );
24      //QUESTION 2
25      this.questions.push(
26          new com.flametreepublishing.QuizQuestion(
27              2,
28              "How many planets are there in our Solar System?",
```

Above: Steps 5 & 6: Add a call to loadQuestions(), as shown here.

5. In a completed quiz application, we might download the question data from a web server, but for simplicity, we're going to hard-code the questions into our SimpleQuiz class. We'll simulate a download by calling the method loadQuestions() – see the illustration above.

6. In the constructor, add a call to loadQuestions(), as in the illustration above. Notice that we do this through the this keyword.

7. SimpleQuiz can now load and store QuizQuestion objects, but we no longer have a way to render all questions (consider that QuizQuestion's renderQuestion method needs to be called from somewhere).

8. Create a new method of SimpleQuiz called renderAllQuestions().

```
44  com.flametreepublishing.SimpleQuiz.prototype.renderAllQuestions = function() {
45      for(var i = 0; i < this.questions.length; i++) {
46          this.questions[i].renderQuestion();
47      }
48  }
```

Above: Steps 7, 8 & 9: This is how to render all questions, as described in the steps above.

9. Within the body of `renderAllQuestions`, create a `for` loop that calls `renderQuestion()` on each QuizQuestion object as in the illustration.

10. Save SimpleQuiz.js and switch to simpleQuiz.html.

```
11      <body>
12          <script type="text/javascript">
13              com.flametreepublishing.simpleQuiz = new com.flametreepublishing.SimpleQuiz();
14          </script>
15
16      </body>
```

Above: Steps 10, 11 & 12: In these steps, you will instantiate SimpleQuiz.

11. Locate the `<script>` element that's within the `<body>` element, and delete the `for` loop – it's now obsolete.

12. Within the same `<script>` block, instantiate SimpleQuiz and assign the instance to `com.flametreepublishing.simpleQuiz`, as shown in the illustration above.

13. Finally, call `renderAllQuestions()` on the newly created SimpleQuiz object as shown below.

```
11
12          <script type="text/javascript">
13              com.flametreepublishing.simpleQuiz = new com.flametreepublishing.SimpleQuiz();
14              com.flametreepublishing.simpleQuiz.renderAllQuestions();
15          </script>
16
```

Above: Step 13: Ensure your HTML page looks like this!

14. Save and close all open files. If you open the page in your browser, nothing will have changed visually, all being well.

THE DOM & EVENTS OF JAVASCRIPT

WORKING WITH THE DOM

Every script we've written so far has worked by outputting data to the page while the page loads. This is OK – but limiting. What if we want to manipulate the page after it has loaded? How do we achieve this?

DYNAMIC HTML

All major browsers support something called Dynamic HTML – or DHTML for short. DHTML allows JavaScript to make changes to a page after it has been loaded and rendered in the browser, with such changes immediately shown on screen. This presents us with a whole host of possibilities – your imagination really is the limit.

```
22
23  /*-----------------------------------------------------------------
24  We've changed checkUserAnswer() considerably - see comments within the body of the
25  method...
26  -----------------------------------------------------------------*/
27  com.flametreepublishing.QuizQuestion.prototype.checkUserAnswer = function(answerIndex) {
28      //Initialise theResult to false - we can change this if the question was correctly answered
29      var theResult = false;
30      if(this.questionAnswered) {
31          //If the question has already been answered then report this in an alert and do nothing more
32          alert("You've already answered this question");
33      } else if(answerIndex == this.correctAnswerIndex) {
34          //If the correct answer is given then mark the question as being correctly answered
35          this.answeredCorrectly = true;
36          //Now set the style class of the question's <div> so that it changes to green
37          document.getElementById("q" + this.questionNum).className = "correctlyAnswered";
38          //And set theResult to true
39          theResult = true;
40      } else {
41          //If the question has been incorrectly answered then change the <div> style class name
42          //so that it has a red background
43          document.getElementById("q" + this.questionNum).className = "incorrectlyAnswered";
44      }
45      //Record that this question has now been answered
46      this.questionAnswered = true;
47      //Now return the result. This isn't actually being used any more, but it's nonetheless
48      //useful to have methods return a result, even if only to indicate that the code was
49      //executed in full without errors.
50      return(theResult);
```

Above: Additional explanations are contained in the downloadable code examples.

Hot Tip

Be sure to download the code examples – see page 13. As well as enabling you to check your code against ours, you'll also find comments included that help to further explain the examples.

HTML IS HIERARCHICAL

All HTML documents contain an `<html>` element; this element always contains a `<head>` and a `<body>` element; these elements themselves contain other elements. A page is, therefore, a hierarchical structure of HTML elements. We express this structure in terms of ancestry: `<html>` is the **root** and has two **children**, `<head>` and `<body>`; `<html>` is the **parent** of `<head>` and `<body>`; `<head>` and `<body>` are **siblings**.

What is the DOM?

We know that JavaScript enables us to create similar hierarchical structures by storing objects within other objects; as it turns out, this is exactly how a web page is represented under the hood of the browser. This representation – or model – is known as the Document Object Model, or DOM for short.

```
<html>
    <head>
        <title>
        A Simple Quiz
        </title>
        <script>
        js/SimpleQuiz.js
        </script>
    </head>

    <body>
        <h3>
        A Simple Quiz
        </h3>
        <div>
            <h3>
            Question 1
            </h3>
        etc.
        </div>
    </body>
</html>
```

Above: HTML elements are nested within other HTML elements; all elements have a parent, and many have siblings and children.

DOM PROGRAMMING

JavaScript's DOM classes, such as HTMLDocument and HTMLElement, provide numerous methods for manipulating a loaded page, and expose properties that directly map to HTML attributes. For example, a <p> element is represented in the DOM by an HTMLElement object. Any attributes defined on the <p> element are available to JavaScript as properties of the corresponding object; any properties defined by JavaScript on the object become attribute values of the <p> element.

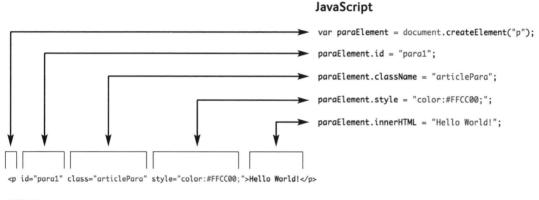

JavaScript

```
var paraElement = document.createElement("p");

paraElement.id = "para1";

paraElement.className = "articlePara";

paraElement.style = "color:#FFCC00;";

paraElement.innerHTML = "Hello World!";
```

```
<p id="para1" class="articlePara" style="color:#FFCC00;">Hello World!</p>
```

HTML

Above: Attributes of an HTML element become properties of the corresponding DOM object, and vice versa.

Retrieving Elements from the DOM

As we've seen, all HTML elements (with the exception of <html>) have to be nested within another element. Therefore, to add a new element to a page with JavaScript, we often have to retrieve the element from the DOM that will serve as the parent of the new element. At other times, we may want to apply, say, a style change to all elements of a certain type.

The methods for getting elements are defined on the single HTMLDocument instance, the top level of the DOM. We have already been using this object in our scripts – every time we type document, we are accessing this HTMLDocument object.

Adding Elements to the DOM

Let's explore DOM programming by updating the QuizQuestion class's `renderQuestion` method.

1. Open QuizQuestion.js in your editor and locate the `renderQuestion` method.

2. Currently, this method uses `document.write` to output a literal HTML string to the page. This technique only works if the method is executed while the page is loading – let's fix that.

```
36
37  com.flametreepublishing.QuizQuestion.prototype.renderQuestion = function() {
38      document.write("<h2>QUESTION " + this.questionNum + "</h2>");
39      document.write("<p>" + this.questionText + "</p>");
40      document.write("<p>A1: " + this.answers[0] + "</p>");
41      document.write("<p>A2: " + this.answers[1] + "</p>");
42      document.write("<p>A3: " + this.answers[2] + "</p>");
43      document.write("<p>A4: " + this.answers[3] + "</p>");
44  }
45
```

Above: This method won't work once the page has loaded.

3. Delete the body of the `renderQuestion` method.

4. On-screen, we're going to lay out each question inside a `<div>` element – the code in the illustration below shows you how to create one. Note that this new `<div>` is not yet part of the page – it's created off-screen, where it stays until it's assigned to a parent element.

```
36
37  com.flametreepublishing.QuizQuestion.prototype.renderQuestion = function() {
38      var questionDiv = document.createElement("div");
39
40  }
41
```

Above: Step 4: `document.createElement()` creates new elements off-screen.

```
36
37  com.flametreepublishing.QuizQuestion.prototype.renderQuestion = function() {
38      var questionDiv = document.createElement("div");
39      questionDiv.id = "q" + this.questionNum;
40      var questionHeading = document.createElement("h2");
41      questionHeading.innerHTML = "QUESTION " + this.questionNum;
42      questionDiv.appendChild(questionHeading);
43
44  }
```

Above: Steps 5 & 6: Continue to build the question's HTML elements, like this.

5. Give the `<div>` an id value derived from the QuizQuestion object's `questionNum` property as in line 39 of the illustration above.

6. We'll create an `<h2>` element to hold the question title; once created, we need to give it some text content using the HTMLElement object's `innerHTML` property, and add it to the `<div>` with `appendChild` – see the illustration above.

7. Use the same techniques to add the text for the question and answers to the `<div>`, as shown in the illustration below.

```
41      questionHeading.innerHTML = "QUESTION " + this.question
42      questionDiv.appendChild(questionHeading);
43      var questionTextPara = document.createElement("p");
44      questionTextPara.innerHTML = this.questionText;
45      questionDiv.appendChild(questionTextPara);
46      for(var i = 0; i < this.answers.length; i++) {
47          var answerPara = document.createElement("p");
48          answerPara.innerHTML = this.answers[i];
49          answerPara.id = "a" + i;
50          questionDiv.appendChild(answerPara);
51      }
52
53  }
```

Above: Steps 7 & 8: This code will build the rest of the HTML elements needed to display the question.

8. Notice that rather than manually typing code for each of the possible answers, we've wrapped this up in a `for` loop that iterates through the `answers` array. Also notice that we've set an `id` attribute for each answer's `<p>` element.

9. Finally, we need to add our `<div>` element to the page. We'll add it to the `<body>` element, which can be accessed with `document.body` as in the illustration below.

10. Save your work and open the page in Firefox. Once again, we see the same thing as before, but this time we have built the page using DOM programming.

```
49      answerParu.tu = u + i;
50              questionDiv.appendChild(answerPara);
51      }
52          document.body.appendChild(questionDiv);
53 }
54
```

Above: Step 9: Add the element to the page, as shown here.

EVENTS

Web pages issue events in response to various conditions and user actions, such as a page having loaded successfully, or the user clicking on something. Responding to these events is one of JavaScript's key roles.

JAVASCRIPT EVENT MODELS

There are a few different event models in JavaScript that have evolved over the years. We don't have space to cover them all, so we'll focus on the current best practice model, known as the W3C model. This isn't the simplest of the models, but it's the one that you should aim to use.

Hot Tip

If you want to explore all of the JavaScript event models, an excellent discussion of them can be found at www.quirksmode.org/js/introevents.html

Left: Quirksmode.org/js/ is a fantastic resource for both new and experienced JavaScript developers.

WHAT IS AN EVENT?

An event is a message issued by the browser. An event always has a type – the type indicates the nature of the event – whether it's a click, a page load, a key press and so on. For example, clicking on any element in a page causes that element to send – or **dispatch** – an event of type "click".

LISTENING FOR AN EVENT

In order to respond to an event, we have to write code that 'listens' for that event occurring – this code is called an **event listener**. When an event listener detects an event of the type it is listening for, it evaluates an expression that performs some action(s) in response to the event.

Above: Events are generated by elements on a page; JavaScript can listen for those events.

Event Handlers

Typically, when an event listener is triggered, the expression it executes is a function or method call. The function or method being called is referred to as an event **handler**. It is the event handler's job to deal with the event in some way – making visual changes, sending data to a server, and so on.

Adding an Event Handler

Our Simple Quiz application needs to be able to respond to the user clicking on an answer – let's define an event handler as a first step.

1. Open SimpleQuiz.js. We're going to create a new method called `clickHandler` – move to the bottom of the document and add the method as shown in the illustration below.

```
59
60  com.flametreepublishing.SimpleQuiz.prototype.clickHandler = function(e) {
61      //click handler statements go here
62  }
63
64
```

Above: Step 1: Add the method as shown here.

2. When using the W3C event model, the event handler is always passed an object containing details about the event – our method captures this as the parameter e. By doing this, we can access the element on which the event occurred by referencing e.`target` as in the illustration below.

```
59
60  com.flametreepublishing.SimpleQuiz.prototype.clickHandler = function(e) {
61      var clickedAnswerId = e.target.id;
62  }
63
```

Above: Step 2: e.`target` references the HTML element that triggered the event.

3. We need to identify the answer that was clicked – this is why our code defines an `id` value for each answer's <p> element. Each answer's `id` is the answer index prefixed by the letter

```
59
60  com.flametreepublishing.SimpleQuiz.prototype.clickHandler = function(e) {
61      var clickedAnswerId = e.target.id;
62      var clickedAnswerIndex = Number(clickedAnswerId.substr(1, 1));
63  }
64
```

Above: Step 3: This code identifies which answer has been clicked.

'a', so we need to access just the second character of the id; we cast this second character to a number because we are going to use it as an index of the questions array. See the illustration above.

4. Note the use of the substr() method of the string class, which enables us to access a section of the string it is called on. The first parameter is the character position that the section starts on (zero-based, like an array index); the second is the length of the section to return.

Above: Step 4: substr() is a method of the String class.

5. Our event handler also needs to know the question number – we can extract this from the <div> element's id attribute. We can access the <div> by referencing e.target.parentNode (the <div> is the parent of the <p>) as in the illustration below.

```
62          var clickedAnswerIndex = Number(clickedAnswerId.substr(1, 1));
63      var clickedQuestionId = e.target.parentNode.id;
64      var clickedQuestionNum = Number(clickedQuestionId.substr(1, 1));
65  }
66
```

Above: Step 5: Extract the question number that has been answered from the event object.

6. Now the handler knows the question number, it can retrieve the corresponding QuizQuestion object from the `questions` array. However, in an event handler, `this` refers to the element that triggered the event, not the object handling the event, so we need to use a global reference to access the `questions` array. The code for this is in the illustration below.

Hot Tip

The `parentNode` **property of an HTML element refers to the parent of that element, i.e. the element in which an element is nested.**

```
59
60  com.flametreepublishing.SimpleQuiz.prototype.clickHandler = function(e) {
61      var clickedAnswerId = e.target.id;
62      var clickedAnswerIndex = Number(clickedAnswerId.substr(1, 1));
63      var clickedQuestionId = e.target.parentNode.id;
64      var clickedQuestionNum = Number(clickedQuestionId.substr(1, 1));
65      var clickedQuestion = com.flametreepublishing.simpleQuiz.questions[clickedQuestionNum -1];
66  }
67
```

Above: Step 6: This code retrieves the QuizQuestion object for the answer that was clicked.

7. Now that we have the QuizQuestion object and answer index that the user clicked, we can determine whether the correct answer was given and report this to the user – this code is shown in the illustration below.

```
65      var clickedQuestion = com.flametreepublishing.simpleQuiz.questions
66      if(clickedQuestion.checkUserAnswer(clickedAnswerIndex)) {
67          alert("Correct! Well done.");
68      } else {
69          alert("No - that's not correct. Try again.");
70      }
71  }
```

Above: Step 7: The code given here will inform the user whether or not their answer was correct.

8. Save your work. Don't open the file in your browser yet – we're not quite finished.

EVENT LISTENERS

Event listeners are assigned to the object that generates the event we want to capture – often this is a DOM object from the web page. Once we know the object we want to listen to, we call `addEventListener()` on that object – the general form is:

`myObject.addEventListener(`*eventType, handlerExpression, useCapture*`)`

Parameters of the AddEventListener() Method

○ **Event type:** The first parameter indicates the type of event to listen for. This is a string such as `"click"`, `"keydown"` or `"mouseover"`.

○ **Handler expression:** Typically a reference to a handler function or method. Note that when referencing a function or method, we do not include parentheses.

○ **Use capture:** This is complex and beyond the scope of the book. Until you learn what this does, always pass `false` to this parameter.

```
1
2  function clickHandler() {
3        //do things in response to the click
4  }
5
6  var myPara = document.createElement("p");
7  document.body.appendChild(myPara);
8  myPara.addEventListener("click", clickHandler, false);
9
```

Above: Adding an event listener to a `<p>` element.

Adding Event Listeners

We've created our event handler, but it doesn't do anything until triggered by an event listener.

1. Open QuizQuestion.js and locate the `for` loop within the `renderQuestion` method.

```
46    for(var i = 0; i < this.answers.length; i++) {
47        var answerPara = document.createElement("p");
48        answerPara.innerHTML = this.answers[i];
49        answerPara.id = "a" + i;
50        answerPara.addEventListener("click", com.flametreepublishing.simpleQuiz.clickHandler, false);
51        questionDiv.appendChild(answerPara);
52    }
```

Above: Step 2: Enter the code shown here as described above.

2. Create an empty line after the one that sets the `answerPara.id` property and insert the code shown in the illustration on the previous page.

3. We don't include the parentheses in the reference to the handler method. If we did, the expression would be evaluated as a method call when the event listener is assigned – we want the expression to be the name of the handler, not a call to it.

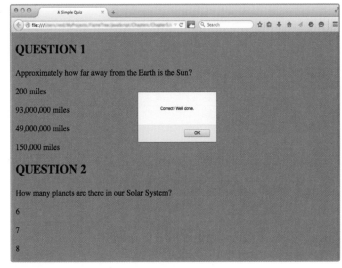

4. Save your work, open simpleQuiz.html in Firefox and click an answer. At last – we have a working quiz.

Above: After all our hard work, we have a functioning quiz.

FINISHING TOUCHES

Let's add one more event listener and handler – they will start the application when the page load completes.

1. Create a new JavaScript document and save it in your project's js folder as quizStartup.js. Enter our namespace declaration at the top of the document.

2. Add the event handler code shown in the illustration on the next page. You should understand it by now – if not, download our code examples and study the comments.

```
 8
 9  com.flametreepublishing.startQuiz = function() {
10      com.flametreepublishing.simpleQuiz = new com.flametreepublishing.SimpleQuiz();
11      com.flametreepublishing.simpleQuiz.renderAllQuestions();
12  }
13
```

Above: Step 2: The event handler code.

3. Add the event listener code shown in the illustration below. The window object represents the browser window – we're listening for its load event, dispatched when the page has finished loading.

```
11          com.flametreepublishing.simpleQuiz.renderAllQuestions();
12  }
13
14  window.addEventListener("load", com.flametreepublishing.startQuiz, false);
15
```

Above: Step 3: The event listener code.

4. Save your work and open simpleQuiz.html in your editor.

5. Add a new <script> element in the <head> and link it to quizStartup.js. Then delete the <script> element that's within the <body> element entirely, and save the file. See the illustration, below.

```
 3      <head>
 4          <title>A Simple Quiz</title>
 5
 6          <script type="text/javascript" src="js/QuizQuestion.js"></script>
 7          <script type="text/javascript" src="js/SimpleQuiz.js"></script>
 8          <script type="text/javascript" src="js/quizStartup.js"></script>
 9
10      </head>
```

Above: Step 5: Ensure you add and delete the right code here.

Next Steps

And that's it – our quiz now works! More to the point, consider what our HTML document contains: just three script elements. JavaScript is handling everything else – nice!

If you want to improve on the quiz game, why not add a style sheet to make things look prettier? You could also take it up a level by recording the user's answers and tracking their score – you have the knowledge to do this. For additional tips though, see SimpleQuiz_onwards in the code examples package.

ONWARDS!

You've taken your first steps into the deep and detailed world of HTML, CSS and JavaScript. You should feel that you have gained a solid overview of the languages and how to use them, but there's still much more to learn...

Happy coding!

Above: Try improving the quiz with some CSS and new functionality. Pack it full of your own questions and test your friends and family.

HTML AND CSS ONLINE RESOURCES

The web provides a vast array of tools, libraries and information to make creating web pages and websites a more productive experience. Here we are going to list some of the more useful resources found online.

HTML RESOURCES

W3C
The World Wide Web Consortium is the body responsible for all web standards. Its site is packed with information from simple guides to deeply technical whitepapers.
w3.org

HTML Goodies
Provides HTML tutorials with online samples.
htmlgoodies.com

Mozilla Developer Network
This resource is run by Mozilla, the creators of the Firefox web browser. It offers a quick introduction to HTML and links to a very comprehensive reference library.
developer.mozilla.org/en-US/docs/Web/HTML

HTML5 Rocks
Lots of articles and tutorials. Aimed at the more advanced user of HTML, but still very useful.
html5rocks.com/en

Code Academy
A great website if you're still quite new to coding. Code Academy allows you to take a beginners online coding course for free. If you want to make sure you definitely understand the basics, this could be for you. It also covers CSS.
codecademy.com/learn/web

HTML Tutorial
An extensive tutorial that provides a lot of information for a beginner.
tutorialspoint.com/html/index.htm

CSS RESOURCES

W3Schools
A comprehensive guide to HTML with examples in each chapter and the option to test your code online.
w3schools.com/css

Above: W3Schools has a host of learning resources

CSS3 Info

The latest news, previews and working examples of CSS3.**www.css3.info**

Zen Garden Designs

A good place to see what can be easily achieved with CSS. It also provides lots of inspiration.
mezzoblue.com/zengarden/alldesigns

CSS Tricks

This is a helpful blog providing informative and helpful tips for CSS.
css-tricks.com

Mozilla Developer Network

This is the incredibly useful CSS reference library run by Mozilla (see opposite page for their HTML version).
developer.mozilla.org/en-US/Learn/CSS

WordPress

Here you can find information on WordPress and CSS. Take a look if you're looking to set up a blog on your website.
codex.wordpress.org/CSS

BEST FRAMEWORKS

Foundation

Touted as 'the most advanced responsive front-end framework in the world', Foundation provides all the components needed for a responsive website.
foundation.zurb.com

Bootstrap

The most popular front-end responsive framework used on thousands of sites.
getbootstrap.com

Skeleton

Another popular framework that is best used for smaller projects.
getskeleton.com

Titan

A simple CSS grid framework for responsive web designs.
ww12.titanthemes.com

YAML

A modular framework to create flexible, responsive and accessible websites. It is used widely.
www.yaml.de

JAVASCRIPT ONLINE RESOURCES

USEFUL WEBSITES

Mozilla Developer Network
This site provides all the nitty-gritty detail of the languages supported by Firefox, and how it works with them. A visit to the JavaScript section provides guides, tutorials, an object and class reference section, and more.
developer.mozilla.org/en-US/docs/Web/JavaScript

The JavaScript Source
This site provides a whole host of code snippets that you can copy, paste and adapt into your own code – and they're all free. Why re-invent the wheel when you can download one somebody already made!
javascriptsource.com

How to Node
If you want to start exploring server-side JavaScript then How To Node is a great resource, full of information and tutorials that will help you on your way.
howtonode.org

W3Schools
A good tutorial for JavaScript, with examples to learn from and quizzes to take that will make your learning interactive.
w3schools.com/js

JavaScript.com
A fantastic interactive website that makes learning the basics of JavaScript fun. It is also great for more advanced developers to keep up with news, libraries and frameworks.
javascript.com

Code Academy
An alternative to the website above is Code Academy's course on JavaScript. It is also a very popular way to learn about JavaScript.
codecademy.com/learn/javascript

JavaScript Kit
This website provides a great selection of resources to help both the novice and advanced coders. With scripts, tutorials and tools there's plenty to help you out.
javascriptkit.com

JavaScript Weekly
Keep up with all the latest JavaScript news and articles here! **javascriptweekly.com**

FURTHER READING

Flanagan, D., *JavaScript: The Definitive Guide*, O'Reilly Media, 2011. Widely considered to be the bible of JavaScript, this book covers all aspects of the language in intricate detail, yet maintains an engaging and accessible style throughout. The book includes a comprehensive reference section describing the properties and methods of all built-in objects and classes.

Zakas, N. C., *The Principles of Object-Oriented JavaScript*, No Starch Press, 2014. The author explores JavaScript, unlocking some of the deepest secrets of the language's inner workings along the way.

Powers, S., *JavaScript Cookbook*, O'Reilly Media, 2015. This book is packed with practical code examples. It is aimed at JavaScript developers with some experience, the 'recipes' cover a wide range of scenarios, and offer fast-track solutions to many coding conundrums.

Duckett, J., *JavaScript & JQuery: Interactive Front-end Web Development*, John Wiley & Sons, 2014. If you're looking to express your creativity through code and want to deepen your knowledge of JavaScript and learn about JQuery then this is the book for you.

Stefanov, S., *JavaScript Patterns*, O'Reilly Media, 2010. This book is certainly for the more advanced user of JavaScript. Written by Stoyan Stefanov, creator of YSlow 2.0, it provides an in-depth look at how to solve problems related to functions, objects and inheritance, among others.

Egges, A., *Building JavaScript Games: for Phones, Tablets and Desktop*, Apress, 2014. If you're looking to expand your knowledge on game programming, this is the book to start with. It provides particular focus on creating games for a touch-based interface.

INDEX